AVOID the VOID

AVOID the VOID

A Struggle for Decency

A Journey from a Soviet Asylum to Paradise Forgotten

GUNNAR GJENGSET, Ph. D.

NEW YORK

AVOID the VOID
A Struggle for Decency
A Journey from a Soviet Asylum to Paradise Forgotten

ISBN 978-1-61448-384-7 paperback
ISBN 978-1-61448-385-4 eBook
Library of Congress Control Number: 2012953817

Morgan James Publishing
The Entrepreneurial Publisher
5 Penn Plaza, 23rd Floor,
New York City, New York 10001
(212) 655-5470 office • (516) 908-4496 fax
www.MorganJamesPublishing.com

Cover Design by:
Brenda Haun
BHaundesigns@gmail.com

Interior Design by:
Bonnie Bushman
bonnie@caboodlegraphics.com

To Anne

TABLE OF CONTENTS

Voluntarily, I walked into a Soviet criminal asylum in the winter of 1970. I left the asylum with a package: A Posttraumatic Stress Disorder (PTSD) that exploded some thirty-five years later, on re–entering the former East Germany. Until then, I had tried to drown what was buried deep inside me, with oceans of alcohol. Slowly I got rid of it all. It took some will.

This is my story

INTRODUCTION

– Do you really want to get sober?

– Do you really want *him* to get sober?

These are the two crucial questions of this book. And if the answer is YES, here comes the quest:

– What's keeping you?

Anyone who has really tried to get sober knows the answer is: **The Void**.

How to Avoid The Void

... is what this book is about. But first, who are you, my reader? Are you one of my two kinds of readers? The abuser, or should I say former abuser, of alcohol, who is about to administer an act of will: to stop drinking. I have one question for you: Do you really want to quit? Because you have to quit – lying, storing, pretending, just–one–for–the–roading, in short: You have to stop drinking. All together. For at least one year. And then you can drink whatever you want to. I can guarantee. Because drinking is not part of your genetic patterns – it is not written in the stars, there is no abusive sequence lurking in your DNA – there are other matters that trigger you. And then there is your will.

The *other* reader is probably the spouse, if there is any. Do you really want him to quit? Or *her*, seldom as it may be – the situation is the same: Do you really want the culprit to quit? The person will alter, and will no longer be dependant. Upon you. You will no longer be in charge. The person will be conducting the person's own will. How fun is that? Are you the loved one, or just the helper? The 'helper' usually helps prolonging the dependence and the abuse – a helpful helper would have posed the ultimate choice: Either stop the abuse, or I leave you. Then up and leave. So, if you really want him to quit, you know what to do. Stop helping, but do not stop reading this book. It might be useful with a visit to the inside of the abuser's mind.

And as you have already observed: The Abuser of this book, your humble dipsomaniac, is a man. So this book's focus is a male one – but this only reflect the usual picture:

> Recent data from the National Institutes of Health reports that 15% of the people living in the United States are considered "problem drinkers." Of this 15%, 5%–10% of the males and 3%–5% of the females could be labeled as alcoholics. Another study found that approximately 30% of people in the United States report experiencing an alcohol disorder at one point in their lifetime. Researchers from the University of California, San Diego have found that the lifetime risk of alcohol–use disorders for men is greater than 20%. They share that there is a risk of around 15% for alcohol abuse and 10% risk for alcohol dependence. (Accessed, July 17, 2012, Alcohol Addiction: http://www.alcoholaddiction. info/alcoholism–statistics.htm).

But, of course, females are also at the risk of developing a dangerous drinking pattern, and most of the time they believe they are cleverer in masking their bad habits: Not so! This only serves to make it more embarassing, perhaps. But they *are* being far more careful than their male counterparts – because men are more inclined to just up and go out on their drinking wives – we are not that compassionate, perhaps. Consequently, tranquilizers and sedatives are more widespread among girls – with an acute hazard of developing a situation of parallel abuse.

So please bear with me, dear lady: If you buy and read this book, the chance is that the impulse was more your boozing spouse than your own intake. But once you have finished reading this book, please leave it on your husband's pillow! It just might work.

To Avoid The Void

But why this abuse? In the Norwegian language one is *full* when one is plastered. It is synonymous with the English word *full,* Merriam-Webster defines it as "containing all that can be held, filled to utmost capacity". You have the urge to fill this horrible void that is consuming you from within. Not just the loneliness; the total emptiness, the lack of substance, the meaninglessness, the *lessness* – wherever you are, with whomever, doing whatever, in the middle of you-know-hat: Everything goes blank, only the stars are yelling at you in their furious soundlessness. *The Void.*

So the use and abuse commences. Of whatever substance. But your choice is alcohol. A legal commodity, for the time being. It comes in a plethora of flavors, but they all have the same effect: It kills you. Somewhat faster than cigarettes, and depending upon your appetite, however, – but it is a slow suicide nevertheless.

There are some exceptions: If you really have no more than 1–2 glass of wine each day, OR a beer, OR a small drink (that is 2,5 cl whisky) per day, you are probably in the clear. But who does? Some civilized individuals, I know. But to be honest, most drinkers change the OR with AND, without noticing. A few of my well–off friends have died on me. As John Lennon expressed so eloquently, "they didn't notice that the lights had changed".

So you continue drowning in the void. But your void is clouded by your growing self–deception, spotted by everyone but you. Then they start leaving you: Your wife (*the bitch!*), your family, your friends, your jobs, your money – and you are yourself taking permanent leave of your senses. But you get some new friends... really helping you not to afford your flat, and the nightmare continues.

Just Quit

We have all been there. That's why you have opened this book. So I will not ponder on the details. But you cannot continue reading unless you can nod to the realities of these last paragraphs: You are a drinker and a liar, but in what way are you leaving Las Vegas? For you are on the verge, just like the character Ben Sanderson in *Leaving Las Vegas.* The only question is:

HOW?

Here is the *other* way. I once asked my good doctor for help to control my drinking. His answer was:

– Why don't you just quit?

You know the shape of my rage – *just quit*? How stupid ... as if I don't know... as if I haven't tried many a time and oft ... and so forth. What a moron! How could he possibly understand the troubles I've seen ... hell, I need a beer!

It **IS** stupid. A most hilarious answer, of course. It can't be that simple. But what if it is? Have you really REALLY tried taking the chance on quitting? After the rather painful process of ridding the body of all the reminiscences of alcohol, why not give soberness a chance? Trust me: It is possible. Not easy, because soon you will find yourself constantly debating.... yourself. And a new meaning will appear to the adage: Something got the better of me. But stay put! Read this book but slowly, and soon I will teach you some useful techniques and then another sober week has passed – you are trying out these other activities, discovering new ones and rediscovering some nice ones from more pleasant days and another week has elapsed and day by day life goes on ... and suddenly you can better understand Lennon: "Life is what happens to you when you are busy doing other things".

Physiologically one just needs five days to totally recover from excessive drinking. Five days. And nights. They are the worst. But after five days you have started digesting, reading papers, noticing the world around you and the people habituating it.... and sleep has found you. By all normal standards you are "well".

But then there is The Void .... Because the quest is not to *stop* drinking, but *not* to *start*. And that is what this book is about. First of all, you must *will* drinking. Admit it! The last time you were sober, you had to will yourself to start drinking. Because: If you bothered to stop, you must have considered the pros and cons: Counting money. Counting bottles. Counting hours – when do I have to be sober again? Then I'll have another pint, and how about the fridge? So I need to bring another six–pack ... So you willed yourself not to stop. Now you must will yourself not to start.

The Art of Not to Start

Having read those few pages is a good start for not to start. Do not go any further unless you have suffered through those first five crucial days. And nights. Then you are welcome aboard. We have to plunge into that massive Void that is awaiting you. So this is a tale of my pilgrimage. It lasted for several years of my life. I lost all my "friends", my job, my family (I had to regain the trust of my children) – my future. So I moved. That's probably the smartest thing you can do: A fresh start in a new city. And ignore the proverb from *I Ching* nr. 48, *The Well*:

"You can change the city, but you cannot change the well". My answer is: The will trumps the well! But you will be challenged each and every day. So I took up the challenge.

You have no choice if you want to conquer *The Void*: This is the one distance you have to walk all by yourself. You need to stop drinking all of a sudden. You have to quit all together for one entire year. After that you can take up therapy, if you can afford it. And the distance is one year at least. After total temperance for a year, I can guarantee that you can drink whatever you like for the rest of your life, without losing control. Nothing less than one year, but for my own part, I did not touch a drop of alcohol for five successive years: Better safe than sorry.

And here comes a piece of advice, for free: Something unpleasant will surface. If not, all your time and money spent on drinking has been a total waste! Well, just think about it, there must be a reason for preferring another bottle over returning to whatever it is you do not want to return to ... But, being sober, you have got plenty of time to deal with it, and thus avoiding the Void! But you can measure it in portions – you have to come to terms with whatever surfaces. In my case, Attention Deficit Disorder (ADD) surfaced ...

Or so I thought. And was told. But as time goes by, day after day, week after week, month by month you slowly start to register the scent of ... flowers, bakeries, perfumes – and the sounds and sights ... and your ability to concentrate upon matters of all kinds improves, and measurably. And while you are busy doing other things, this whole idea of ADD or whatever explanation you needed, fades away, until one day you notice that you left them at the bakery ... or perhaps the library ... Whatever! You have tossed away the crutches.

Personally I did not notice the metamorphosis until some time afterwards: I had this intense and persevering aching in my stomach. It would not go away. It was like waiting for something exciting to happen: An exam; you are one cipher away from the ten million win in the National Lottery; will your daughter be accepted at that college; is the off license still open ... you know, this sizzling excitement that is absorbing you from within. Only it is there all the time, but a drink or two would easily – and there you go. I had to administer all my will, and keeping myself busy at all times, watching idiotic programs on the telly, or even visit the movies – and suddenly one day it wasn't there. Gone completely! As was my assumed ADD.

The explanation is that for quite some time, you are engaged in some compensatory businesses, but you do not want to replace abusing alcohol with another abuse. So for some months you will be trying out other activities, until you find yourself settled in an armchair, reading a paper and wondering about tomorrow's weather. And noticing that the nagging feeling in you abdomen is ... well, just not there anymore. When did that happen? But before you reach some answers, there is this ad in the paper about ... and life as we know it is restored.

But before you get there, you have to conquer the Void. Sometimes it is driving you insane, and all it takes to fill it is – you know so well. Fill up the glass! Flee from the pain. That is our nature! To survive, to protect, to avoid discomfort, and the solution you know so well and that has served you so well .... A pint of Oblivion, if you please ... But you have promised to stay sober for a year, so The Void creeps into the outskirts of your consciousness, its growing on you and revealing it's emptiness – you have to fill it, you have to ... DO NOT DESPAIR! But in the months to come, you will try several avenues of occupying your mind. Some will last for a week or two, some others will stay with you for some time, until suddenly you have moved along and are no longer chasing butterflies ...

First of all: Take up some sort of work, if it is available, and if you for some reason are out of work. If not, create some routines, AS IF you are in business. That leaves you with no more than eight hours of The Void a day. But how to deal with them? I will show you. To start with, read this book, hopefully you can learn something about creating some sort of structure out of sheer mess, and structure shall be the mainstay of your new reality.

You might of course frequent a psychotherapist during this first year, if you like and can afford it – but in my experience that may slow down your journey into your own self: After all, you are paying the therapist to sooth you, and if she says what the heck – have a drink! ... you get my drift? See a therapist if that is your choice, but do tell her that for the time being you are enjoying soft drinks for a year, and why, and there you go! She may or may not back you, but she will NEVER challenge a choice that is yours.

But the general idea is to stay sober for a year. Then you are free to drink whatever you choose forever after. Some organizations will challenge this idea. They will claim that you can never again touch a drop, but rather attend to their meetings and read their pamphlets and buy their books and making all these contributions ... This might function for a large number of people. But you might want to find out for yourself.

Reading my book might be helpful. I have really been out on a limb, but still I made my way back to a more sustainable, and much more agreeable, reality. And I enjoy every second of it! And so does my wife, my new and old friends, my children and my grandchildren, of course: They have never experienced me under the influence! Or the other way round: If I hadn't quit, I would never have experienced my grandchildren: Their mothers would simply not have let me. So welcome to my history of ...

Asylum, Addiction and the Road to Avoid The Void

The first part of this book is about this journey to my *Heart of Darkness* – we must all conquer our Congo within. I got there. Almost. So when the question about my possible ADD surfaced, I called upon an old friend, Peter. We met for a talk, and I agreed upon setting a goal for my journey: I should complete the dissertation I once had been working on. I had flunked with a Ph. D.'s thesis on another subject, in another city – in another life. The idiots of the academic committee did not accept it, my friends laughed, my family exchanged glances ... I fled. So now, some fifteen years later, I started afresh, did some heavy reading, started writing, got my supervisor at another university in another country ... but would

I really prevail? Or just stumble into the well? The other thing we agreed upon was for me to trust my own will. Good Old Will. I told Peter about the good doctor who had challenged me with his: "Why don't you just quit?" He laughed and reminded me about this ancient biblical wisdom that faith can Move Mountains, but a more contemporary interpretation would be that it's all a question about will.

And I really completed the new thesis for my Ph. D. But was it accepted? Or to be more precise: Did I really have the self–confidence needed to present it to a scientific commission? I mean – whom was I trying to fool? Was this really I? Or had I just become a product of some ambitious therapists and scholars? Was this assertion really a product of my own will?

You see where I am going? How about my own will? First I had to make a detour – there was a door I had briefly recognized in my soberness–therapy, and quickly passed by. Now I had to open it. Behind that door I will find myself in an asylum, a penitentiary for the mentally deranged – in the former Soviet Union. Remember the USSR? The old Empire of Evil, the Soviet Union. So in the first part we are *Back in the USSR*.

The next part of this book is about my recent journey into the Congo of my inner wits. I am talking about my years in self–therapy, while I was building my new Self – constructing myself. With a little help from my friends, represented by my companion Pyotr in the Soviet asylum. And Peter afterwards. These talks are rendered in Part Two: *A Day in the Life*. We talked about how I started drinking, how much I lost, how to realize one's status as a drunkard. Regardless of income, status and standing – a drunkard you are! This is the hardest bit – it took me twenty years to see that obvious fact. If you survive that part of my book, you are entitled to some practical advices on how to arrange and furnish your re–born existence. How to Avoid The Void. These you will find in Part three: *Norwegian Wood – Avoid the Void*. Hang in there!

Part One:

BACK IN THE USSR

INTRODUCTION:
AN EX–ALCOHOLIC IN
THE EX–SOVIET UNION

There is an explanation for almost everything, and a diagnosis for almost anything. But ADD?

One of the doctors I visited during my years of recovery suggested that I suffered from ADD. What I knew in advance about ADHD or ADD, is that there is a strong academic disagreement about the cause of the condition. Physicians are talking about genetic causes, while psychologists are talking about dysfunctional families. Others deny the existence of such a syndrome. I do not judge, but after the initial giddiness of getting a diagnosis I went into a prolonged mourning. Imagine what I could have accomplished in this world, if ...? I broke down, strangely enough in two phases. In the final phase everything unraveled, and I became psychotic. It did not help the least that I lived right on Las Ramblas in Barcelona. Gaudi's whimsical houses across the street were only a silent reflection of my inner chaos: Life is not a bit as it looks! But the train had begun to wobble dangerously on the track earlier that summer, on visiting the eastern parts of Germany – former DDR – *Deutsche Demokratische Republik*, once run by the same maniacs that erected The Berlin Wall ... that lasted until 1989.

SMACK! A heavy iron door closed behind me on board the car ferry F/S Sassnitz in July 2004. We were on our way to Trälleborg from Sassnitz, my wife Anne and I. As I was well into my first year of temperance, my mind was constantly playing all sorts of tricks on me. Mind games that I usually filed away as part of a restart of my senses, faculties and capabilities. But on our visit to the German isle of Rügen, I suddenly realized that we actually were in the middle of the former Eastern Germany, The German Democratic Republic –*Deutsche Demokratische Republik*. Our last days' journey through the ancient Hanseatic cities was over, but the tingling turmoil was not over. It rose far above the shores of my usual anxiety; this permanent feeling of chaos that I can just slip away from in short glimpses. On the contrary, it bit harder against the backbones, pulling my forgotten images back into focus for some nanoseconds and lighting up dark images that no one should carry around. But what kind of images, which bit of the past was I staring at without recognizing it? *Déja vû.*

Chaos tearing away the foundation under my legs. I am balancing on the thwart of a rowboat, there! confidence sinks to the bottom, and there! rocket to the sky. But where is the balance on the other side? What is it like to balance security? The result is chaos, chaos soaring out from nowhere. It's like a movie from a beautiful summer day, all is peace and harmony, but then there is this scary music humming below and you know ... here it comes!

Since we left beautiful Lübeck this music has been whispering weirdly in the back of my head. The landscape drifted by, and we visited one of the beautiful Hanseatic cities after the other, but something was not right.... So, on the ferry from Sassnitz ...

Smack! The slamming of an iron door behind me, and suddenly the memories fell into place: I was back in my cell in Kuybysjev criminal asylum in Leningrad, in January 1970. Now I was there again, thirty-four years later, and a while after, nearly unconscious, my wife was checking us in at a sumptuous hotel room in Lund, Sweden. It reminded me a bit of the pampering communist party's VIP room at the Finlandia Station in Leningrad. And the day after, around Falkenberg somewhere, I got a sharp attack of anxiety when she left me for a short while in a department store. I was back in *Gostinnyj Dvor*, the largest department store in Leningrad, on Nevsky Prospekt. Outside it was winter and slush, and in a few minutes I would go out on the gallery and throw flyers over the citizens, shouting *Mir drusjba – Peace and friendship*, and expect a harsh treatment of the Soviet state power apparatus.

But all around me there was this fair Swedish summer, peace and harmony, and Anne arrived safely around the corner. The troll was swaying with their heads in mere disappointment, and muttered so only I could hear it: we've got you under surveillance! We'll grab you at our will, we are always around ... There was something strange with this feeling of permanent unrest. I had finished this childish playing with my life like when I demonstrated against Brezhnev, had really taken up some serious careers. In plural. What bothered me was the question: Why did I go to Leningrad? What in heavens name makes young persons volunteer by putting their lives at stake? There must be something wrong with me. Normal people do not act like that.

Our trip through the former East Germany had brought back the memories of locked prison doors, and they were unpleasant. Had I been looking for some hidden rooms in my childhood when I voluntarily played with my life in Leningrad? Suddenly I got the feeling of standing in front of the last locked door of my life. My life had been one long escape away from this door, although I had always returned to it, without seeing it clearly? My whole life had been an escape, an amok–run through a chaotic landscape.

Huge and menacing was the last door in front of me now: You're not able to continue with your life before you open it up, the multiheaded troll whispered from behind the door.

The troll had showed up once we left the Lübeck. We chose to take off from the *Autobahn*, and followed a normal road of poor Norwegian standard to the city of Wismar. It was like driving straight into the past. At first it was charming; the hanseatic city is preserved as a small piece of jewelry from the past. Most of the wall around Wismar was preserved, the macadam in the streets was huge crescents impossible to walk on, and the cars ran on share despite. We stayed at the Alter Speicher Hotel, an all–out Western establishment. Did you spot the troll? *Western* hotel ...?

We dined outdoors in a huge city square that evening. I sensed the peace, but also a little danger. The cars were creeping along the cobbled streets as well as they could, the characteristic jagged ridges of the roofs circled the square, and I had noticed that here you could get haircuts and manicure for five Euros. At the same time, the hair salon served as a gallery and a cafe for ... yes, for whom? The unrest rose: We were sitting amidst a beautiful backdrop, where social deprivation made the unemployed serve cheap coffee and haircuts for five Euros in a gallery that probably was sponsored by the government. We found ourselves in an area with an unemployment rate up to twenty percent, we found ourselves in...

No, I was not ready to take in that I was in an area that I, before the iron curtain crumbled, had been expelled from for life. Only two days later, in horrible Rostock, this dawned on me, though not completely. But I knew that I had here been before. That is to say: In such a place I had been before. We were looking over the Rostock harbor, and munched on a lunch that we had stolen at the Alter Speicher. There was something ominous in the original 1950s warehouses. Hopelessly dilapidated, and sloppy, as if the workers did not give a damn. As a former sailor, I know a lot of warehouses, and the likes of these, I had seen before. Namely when I called at ports in the Soviet Union already in 1964.

When we walked back to the city, we strolled down the main street. A stern and straight naked avenue with a width as the entire Spoon Hill, surrounded by strict brick buildings with just enough stories to make us feel intmidated. At the end there was a palace–like building, with appropriate balconies from which powerful people could wave to the masses. Exactly like *Ulitsa Gorkova*, the avenue leading to the Red Square in Moscow.

It is funny how the brain works sometimes; it refuses to recognize what we are staring at. A kind of self–defense, an autopilot that overrides common sense. Just try walking down an escalator that is not working, it's almost impossible to shuffle your feet properly. My sense realized that we were in East Germany, a place that no longer existed anywhere but in the language. But the same brain would not let me recall that this concept had a special significance for me. We were in *Germany* now, you fool! Huge billboards for McDonald's and Wall–Mart reminded us of that, but what we saw around us was, at best, Germany twenty years ago. We were trapped in a time machine!

The area we went through was like a picture of my own fractured mind: Under a seemingly calm surface, one tries to hide the traces of generations of lies and concealments. With a sudden regime change in 1989, the East German wall opened against the rest of the world. I voluntarily put my past life on hold when I walked into a cell in Leningrad in 1970. But the former East German society are reluctant to take the plunge, the whole atmosphere is charged with the contradictions between the desire to experience the new reality, and the need to retain the old security founded on repression.

Now it was obvious for me: This is how I have felt since 1970. It was not against the Brezhnev oppression I had demonstrated in Leningrad, but against knowledge about a childhood that I had repressed. And the ever–consuming feeling that something was wrong with me, and that no one could enlighten me.

We drove through small towns of inexpressible sadness, miles of residential barracks and a couple of small palaces, beautifully located overlooking the city. And always the best places reserved for the past party bosses, and a massive People's House for the rest of the people. Everywhere a People's House. We drove into Rügen, and settled in a small private hostel in Sassnitz. Every other house was of that sort. It reminded me of the former Yugoslavia: A sort of private capitalism within a communist framework. Down at the harbor lay the entire fishing fleet out of circulation, and almost all ships were restored into restaurants of various kinds. Nobody could make a living from this, of course, and we found ourselves in a society where all cut one another's hair for five Euros. The community around us looked like reality, but was not. We found ourselves in a project, not in a country, and I felt very uncomfortable.

The next day it would be even worse. We went to Prora. It is Europe's longest building. Out on the sand dunes of Rügen the Nazi regime had constructed one of their most sinister memorials. It is a six–story apartment building with a continuous length of four kilometers! In normal walking, it takes forty minutes to walk along this insanity. For approximately every forty feet, there is a transverse staircase. The entire complex consists of 9,855 rooms that can accommodate 20 000 people. This was Hitler's dream of *Kraft durch Freude* (health through pleasure).

We parked outside and on the way down to the prison–like building, I started automatically to glance over my shoulder. Is there any escape? For this was a prison. It stretched as far as we could see and even longer to each side: it was as if the flanks joined together around us, as if the long tube slowly closed the ring behind us. Anyone who has been inside a prison, has got the prison inside. You are free but not free, and now we walked directly into one voluntarily. But this is not a prison, argued Anne, it has never been a prison. She knows little about the character of a prison, so "voluntarily" I went into Prora.

Then *bang!* the closing doors of a prison cell behind me, but none of the others heard anything. I looked carefully around, but no: The others were obviously not bothered by the noise of the doors. The walls were just as puke–green as in a prison, a smell of wet cement, earth, and I heard the desperate cries of lonely people. It was a *Trabi* there, the East Germany manufactured car, funny small effects from Communist Eastern Europe everywhere: Posters who told me about how nice it had been under the regime of General Secretary of the East German Communist Party Walter Ulbricht, because there was a regime of unity and effort. But not a word about the Stasi. We could buy T–shirts with hammer and sickle and *CCCP.* (Cyrillian letters, should be read SSSR: *Soyuz Sovietskih Sotsyialistiychyeskih Respublik*, the United Soviet Socialistic Republic). Pure and simple *ostalgi*, of course, but I felt sick and had to get out. Anne sensed my discomfort, and I tried to explain. But how to explain that Prora actually was a sleeping troll, who was about to devour us?

I felt uncomfortable and wanted to get away, but I did not know from what. My verdict was given in the Leningrad City Court in February 1970 – I was sentenced to one year's imprisonment in a correcting camp, and expelled from the Soviet Union and all countries that had agreements with the Soviet Union, in practice the entire Eastern Block minus Yugoslavia – for life. Yugoslavia was, as I recall, a cheerful country, which I actually had visited voluntarily in the Tito period. It gave me a kick: You and I, Tito, we did defy Soviet!

True, East Germany closed down in 1989, but that was only on paper. There we were at the ferry landing in Rügen in 2004, experiencing how the spirit from the Communist regime prevailed in the heads of bureaucrats, the former *Parteigenossen,* members of the Communist party. Just listen:

We obediently parked at the proper place, and would smoothly go with the next ferry, seemingly. But reality is never as it seems in totalitarian regimes. So when the ferry arrived and cars began to embark, suddenly secret queues of vehicles were waved on board before us. We, however, were not; we were simply left behind. Enraged, I drove up to the ticket booth and asked what the hell! The lady explained very briskly that we had not reserved seats. It is very easy to be angry in German, an excellent language for this state of mind: Why in the names of all the ancient Teutonian gods had she not informed us about the reserved seats? And when might we expect to be welcomed on board?

But the ticket lady could not answer that one.

So I went to the port office of the ferry company, but they had no office here. By now I had become very Eastern Bloc in the head. On the way to the Harbor Office I sensed the watchtowers grow up on the quayside. Barbed wire grew on top of the barriers for cars, and in the booth there was a soldier fully armed with an AK-47 in his lap. Along the fences were soldiers patrolling with machine guns on their shoulders and dogs on a leash. Suddenly, I was transported aboard a train. Outside the window stood a watchtower all by itself. I went out into the corridor and then spotted another watchtower, no, two. Along the rails were soldiers, they raised the guns and had a snarling German shepherd dogs in chains.

Slightly confused, I shook my head. There were no guard towers, but some train tracks that stretched right into the ferry, and it struck me that this harbor would have been the place for many a watchtower. And whole lot of army barracks, to make sure to discourage any thought of escaping to the West. The Harbor Office was built as a watchtower, even if it was completely new. It is not easy to put down old aesthetics, I thought, as I eased my way to the Information.

I found it, but got no information. Why did not anybody inform us that we had to book a ride? When can we expect to go, now that we are first in line? How should we acquire a valid ticket? Too complicated to answer, of course. When I dared forward a complaint, the officials simply turned their backs on me! I suppressed the rage, and horrified I thought that a few years ago they might have shot me. Or something a little less drastic. But they were not allowed staging such responses anymore, and in pure powerlessness over a new situation where government officials had been deprived of all the power they previously could lean on when torturing others, they just turned their backs on me.

I called the shipping company in Sweden and arranged the ferry ticket. The woman in the ticket booth appeared flat out disappointed, and suddenly we were on board the next ferry. I stood on deck and looked toward the guard towers that were not there, train huffed on board, some ship–hands checked wheels of the compartments, seals and such, and there were no military with German shepherd dogs in Viborg. Viborg? Had I ever been to Viborg in the Russian Karelia, and by train? Thoughtful, I strolled across the deck, and Anne was full of admiration of how I had coped with the bureaucracy here, and I thought to myself, if you only knew! *At the risk of my life!* No, this was Boobs Show, we were safe in the modern reality now, and certainly our contemporary reality was no further away than a mobile call, but: Was it reality, we had just been visiting? We opened the iron door and went inside from the deck. The door slammed into place behind us, and *smack*! I was back in his cell in Leningrad. But how come?

1

A DAY IN THE
LIFE OF GUNNAR
GJENGSETOVITSCH

— *Kurrits, basjalst!* Out and smoke!

The cell door rattled against the wall, the entire Russian army filled the open door and slowly winter winds seeped into my room. I have to call it my "room" – otherwise it is a ... well, you know. When they close the door it is my *room*, although it is a cell from the outside. For here I sit. And it's just me who know how it is here. And here is my room.

But now I'm outside. Today's diversion and absolute highlight. Two time boys enter my cell with the equipment I need between my pajamas and the Russian winter. First the foot–cloths: rags to wrap around the foot before you drag the boots on. After three days I have learned to wrap them properly, it is important that not a touch of the skin is open and carry the cold to the rest of the body. Then a couple of canvas trousers, and so my legs are inserted into the felt boots. And then even more felt on the outside, depending on the temperature. For I am in Leningrad, still Leningrad, this crazy Venice copy where hundreds of thousands got stuck for life in the marshes and swamps. Short lifetime: the city is built on marshes and bodies.

The weather changes as a winter in Trondheim, my Norwegian hometown. Today: Cold. I'm going to freeze my fingers. No gloves, no pockets. Why no pockets in no clothes? Are they afraid that I'm going to strangle myself with a pocket? Better yet with the cold rather than the mild weather. There are no soles on these boots, the felt absorbs the puddles and I carry half the Gulf of Finland into the cell. Excuse me: Room.

So out. I have all the yard alone. I'm not just crazy, I'm also a political prisoner. And it is known that such a diagnosis is highly contagious. I walk around a bit and blink against the bright light, feel weak and empty and weak and empty. And hungry. Terrifyingly, gut wrenching hungry. But still only the third day on the hunger strike, just water without bread thank you very much, the third or fourth day? and I make a note that I must find a way to keep track of days so that if you shall perish you should know what day it happens, it is not at all uninteresting if there is on the 17th , 19th , or 43rd day! But perishing was not planned. There is a line between idealism and suffering. Later, I learned that idealism is false consciousness.

So I starved. And had learned that the first three of four days are the worst. I was welcome to help myself, said my host, no one in the West had heard about me and why would the newspapers write about me, a young and confused student who had been tricked by tsarists, revengers, Nazi collaborators and agents of the Soviet enemy number one, the exile organization NTS. And sumptuous bowls and plates filled my room and were brought in with alarming frequency. The scents growing intensely the moment I closed my eyes, but I shook off my illusions and thought of Chaplin in *The Gold Rush*, at least he had shoelaces!

I am not allowed to smoke either, actually. But already the second day the prison *trustee* must surely have thought that hell, all Russians smoke, and he's just a confused neighbour who must be met with our hospitality!

I got to taste the *Papyrusski*. A smoking device where almost two thirds of it is a mouth piece of cardboard, and where it must be held horizontal, to prevent the tobacco from sprinkling out of the... You get the idea. The tobacco was as dry as a cigarette you took from where you left it two years ago. And yet I have said nothing about the smell.

But the taste was heavenly.

Peaceful minutes in free air. Around me, barbed wire everywhere. Like in a small cage we were chugging along slowly, one hand in the other armpit while five frozen fingers hover around the smoke. Foot–rags are keeping the heat well enough, but I wonder if this is a surplus from the GULAG, undeniably it seems degrading to have to use rags instead of clothes, and I make a note – this I have to check afterwards. Is this a typical Russian or typical GULAG habit?

For there will be a time for afterwards, but the plan was to provoke a lawsuit, the plan was to keep out of any prison camp until the pressure from the West became too annoying. It was what we had worked for: small but numerous and annoying pinpricks, demonstrations and noise – now I was about to launch the main stunt. And everything seems to work, several days have passed – three or four? – And I'm still here. According to the plan.

A smoking hunger artist in a cage. Peacefully under a clear sky which bears a slight shimmer from Helsinki. In the middle of St. Petersburg, Peter the Great's insane dream of Europe, of ice free waterways away from the Turks and Mongol hordes. And strolling shoulder to shoulder with the Red Army ... my personal sentry, a private soldier who seems to be ashamed of carrying this rifle around but he is the guy who has *spitsjki* (matches). My life's first teacher in Russian. For far away from the prison management and politics we mumble little secrets about Grieg and *Ch*amsun – they have plenty of s–es in Russian, but *h* they do not have! – Nansen he knew of naturally, but it is Hamsun first and last, and he is mounting his entire knowledge of German and exclaims:

– *Wir Lieben ja Chamsun!*

Maybe someone has seen us. For I see him no more, thinking that maybe they thought they had found a suitable ignorant and silly soldier, forgetting that every true Russian loves Hamsun. Anyway, he was removed, perhaps placed in less pleasant barracks and I think that it is a shame how much trouble that splendid but condemned author still was able to bring about.

Half an hour is over.

I shuffle my legs into the cell, the boys are very respectful towards this strange bird that has crash–landed here and offer me my toilet visit out of turn. No toilet in the room, not easy to deal with such a situation. I am equipped with carefully measured paper and should have fathomed the unbelievable luxury they equip me with – but all I understand is that they call it *bumagi* and is something I need to use for a completely different mission. Writing this book, for instance ...

So The Room: It is approximately three square meters. A bed with mattress and a blanket. Nothing more. But I'm alone. The bars give a notion of the old city jail of Oslo, the capital of Norway, but behind them you can actually just open a window for an inch or two. Between window and the bars there is a niche that will prove to be most welcome. The window is located partly below ground level, I can only see a whole lot of bricks neatly stacked up as a wall, no sky, no trees, no nothing. But just outside the walls meanders Leningrad. Odor of poorly refined gasoline is seeping in, tram screeches and reveals roughly what time of day we have. Otherwise, I always know when the clock is precisely 0600 in the morning. The Russian National Anthem is playing over the intercom, and the light is turned on?

The light is not turned on, because it is not turned off. *Never.* The light is in the ceiling. Around the clock the light is on in the ceiling, and there is no angle where one can escape the light. I have tried with the blanket over my head, but then immediately someone says something that surely means blanket away from the head, thank you! Maybe they think that I might commit a quick little suicide under the blankets, swallow my tongue or any other commando tricks that they have heard secret agents are doing when cornered.

For they can see me all the time. The owner of the eye in the door has a small metal flap in front of him on the outside, I can hear every time they take a look. And this was How I learned to love the Russian National Hymn. Someone claimed, give me a fixed point. I have found mine. The National Anthem sounds, the world is back on hinges. The time is again set in motion.

Time is heavy when empty. My head is full of all sorts of things and nowhere to put it. Nothing to read, but curiously enough on day two I got the current copy of the *Leningradskaya Pravda*. One of the guards (guards being of a different stature than the boys that are doing time themselves) preached rather maliciously as he underlined one title with his index finger:

– *Fi–as–ko Gonnare Gjongseta*

Interestingly use of vowels, but there you go. Never has any newspaper headline made me so happy, for I had learned the Cyrillic alphabet.

But they must have known, for after having stumbled my way painstakingly through the article I was able to understand quite a lot of – amazing how Latin has spread – and before I was able to continue with a bulletin about speed skating, big in both Soviet and Norway, then swoosh! The newspaper was swept away ...

Given over to my own thoughts. Wondering why the hell do I sit here? Alone on a cot with lights everywhere and all the time and a language that is rambling around with words I do not understand and have the world left me out, or is it me who have joined a different reality and was that really so smart? What incident started this film, was it my immature flirt with certain right wing ideas, fear of communism at the gates perhaps, or love of the Russian culture or maybe the love and grief we feel, we who was constipated in the rush of liberation in May 1945 – still longing for those millions of postwar fathers hovering over a stranded prewar automobile and pondering whether it was the pinion this time or maybe the distributor? But all they want is really a time machine.

But all this has to be written down. I ask for *bumagi* but not for a visit to the toilet thank you and show them that I want to write and make a hell of a fuss and the boys get the guards to get hold of the trustee – he's my man! and this man thank God knows a little German, but paper? for writing? Prisoner's conditions should be made as unbearable as they dare and what use do I have for paper and a gift for lying is vital:

– I'll write my confession.

He looks at me and understands. He looks disappointed and do not understand so I have to blink a little hoping that perhaps he understands, and suddenly ignition in his eyes:

– Aha! Confession! *Aber sofort*!

He explains that it might take some time, the director has gone for the day (he is called Smirnoff as the vodka, and so are almost all the Russians), but tomorrow, tomorrow morning even he, Sergei Ivanovich himself . . .

Happily I lie down on the bed, ignoring the walls, they are green, a color I later called intestine green and think happy thoughts about life at sea, on top of a mountain, or anywhere else but ...

2

MOTHER RUSSIA

Nothing started in 1968.

There were a lot of full stops, but we started nothing. The Communists saved de Gaulle, the Communists will have a rematch in Czechoslovakia and in Germany Rudi Dutschke was shot. And that meant the end of The Great Conversation. Shots fired in the East and West and soon not a single enemy to be found that we can count on. We are in The Age of Coincidences.

And suddenly the year was 1969. A parade of Men is stepping in and out, but also one Woman: Golda Meir becomes prime minister of Israel. Otherwise, Dubcek out and Lin Piao in edge to edge with Willy Brandt and Pompidou, de Gaulle out of the row. Adorno dies the same year as Woodstock, and here is a dual symbolism for anyone who dares: The philosopher Adorno and all his cousins were out on the scene of the so–called Youth Rebellion, but Adorno was also a musician. The philospher Herbert Marcuse ruled, and we all belonged to the renown Frankfurter School: Critical philosophy was our aim. Totally out of interest to us someone was landing on the moon but we believed that was an exaggerated show to keep us from doing whatever we had in mind to do.

Jan Palach set himself on fire January 16.

The first meeting took place in July 1969. A whole generation is slowly seeping into collective youth apathy, everywhere around us the ancient faces of granite are jamming the sight. *Franco* lives and rather splendidly in Spain, thank you very much, and colonel Pattakos have learned nothing from the heroic Greek struggle against fascism during the World War II. *Brezhnev* is teetering around on the balustrades of the Kremlin and has reduced himself to two facial expressions: one for normal and one when he sneezes. Brezhnev seldom sneezes.

At the same time, there is a certain amount of traffic to the Soviet Union – young people from several western European countries, creating noise and interference in major magazines and newspapers. A friend of mine was the last activist. He and a Swedish girl got expelled for having handed out leaflets in the Tsum mall. They are high up on a gallery on each side of an atrium and allow the leaflets to snow down into the atrium, the police behaved like idiots blocking the stairways to the galleries and the entire mall, after which thousands of Moscow'ers were whirring around, thrilled by this greatest of all the street theaters: Protesters chaining themselves to the balustrade. And the police cannot cut the cuffs, hundreds of people running up and down inside the enclosed galleries, a massive and rhythmic cheering to keep up the spirits for our heroes and the police need to cut lengths of the railing instead and they have some great efforts towing demonstrators with handcuffs plus railing down the stairs. And the elevators are out of order. As usual. And the headlines are getting bigger and bigger.

One really wants to make a difference.

I got invited to Oslo by a fellow activist after his return from Tsum the mall and his demonstration there. So how come this poor student can pay for my trip to Oslo? Plans are already made and I was already a part of them. The main actor was *I*, but I did not know. Already, two of my closest friends were in Moscow for a recon of the terrain, doing some research on what was working and what wasn't, studying theater programs, making phone calls, investigating who it was possible to make contact with. The whole apparatus was ready, oiled and cleaned. No more beating around the bush. Buckling the trap. Sending me in there and *smack!* the cell door shut. Yet there is much I did not know about. Many other happenings will take place at the same time, both in the Soviet Union and elsewhere in Europe, but into the trap I will walk and setting the game afoot.

3

RIDING THE RAP

Somewhat groggy on a Saturday morning I was asked rather bluntly if I would like to go there for myself to demonstrate. One is asked to dance, to travel the world, and already I have been treated in places I've never heard of. And with tiny briberies: Flights to Oslo were not just a piece of cake at that time. It WAS the cake. With whipped cream and icing and all the trimmings ... But that didn't matter: I had been a sailor. I had seen the world. I was asked to play a role, however only an understudy, it will not pay off but that certainly did not matter. They had no use for idealists, what they needed was a high sensation seeker. My Russian training officer Mike once asked me why I really wanted to do this? And I replied to honour Nabokov, and he was pleased.

But back to the 1970s. I have received a couple of trips from people I have not yet met, Harald and I are talking about the courier business, the dangers and temptations of dissimulation. Free trip to the Soviet Union and the collected works of The Hardy boys' performed entirely on my own, and yet they did not mention the five minutes of world fame. Wise of them. I could have said no. Otherwise, I had already been in the Soviet Union, in Leningrad as a sailor a few years earlier, and that was certainly no disadvantage.

On the whole, I was an excellent agent for them. Single in the world and unconcerned as it goes, no troublesome employer and the only thing I cared for at the moment was student politics in Trondheim. Adventurous as all at my age, but already with a shred of understanding about this life not being such a big deal. Already somewhat weary.

So I met George for the first time. In a tiny hotel room in Oslo, he enters with a little piece of Russia, pronounced *Russia* – he has pickles and vodka under one arm and black bread under the other, we sit down. Harald is there for half an hour and then disappears.

We talked about absolutely nothing. He sat there with his mournfully sagging moustache, a few drops of vodka was always left in the right part of the mournful one, he sucks his mustache and taught me a something about vodka. He spoke very disparagingly of *Moskovskaya*, here in Norway the unconditional purchase would have to be *Stalitsjnaja,* but nothing could compare with the one you cooked yourself, really strong homespun, *vodka krjepki* meaning hotashell and you must always have some snacks to go with it. Something salty; black bread, small sausages or as now: the whole pickled cucumbers. A little bit with each sip. The advantage: not getting drunk for hours. But soon the paradox appeared: how to make the drink last in times of meager means? There are many techniques. Firstly, use glasses as small as possible, preferably thimbles. In the prison camps, he said casually, in the camps we used straws from the grass of the vast Russian plains. Sucked through the fine capillaries one could get lovely drunk on almost nothing.

– Couldn't you just not eat? I wondered. He looked at me with an incredulous look, bordering on disgust. When later I was reading Sholokhov's *And Quiet flows the Don*, I understood better. This leading writer–icon of the Soviet state was flying high on a book in which the Soviet people is displayed with insult, for those who can read. Then I realized what George was hinting about: The Russians are not a people, they are a paradox.

I surfaced from these meetings but had gathered nothing, and learned a lot. About how important it was to learn the Cyrillic alphabet: I had to be able to read street signs, damn it! Without teaching me anything we sauntered in his virtual version of Moscow. I could *see* Lenin Hill from every angle, down town was the Kremlin with all its domes, the main street was called *Ulitsa Gorkova* and all signs began with *Ul., street.* We walked through the Arbat, the old workers' quarters that now mostly housed artists, intellectuals and others suspect individuals, no street signs there but from where large quantities of *samizdat,* the underground newspapers, were printed and distributed.

– Samizdat means something like "self-publishing", George explained.

– Underground Press, like the illegal papers you probably had during the war. Any owner of a typewriter is a publishing house, news are printed and five–six copies are finding their way to someone owning a copier and before you know the word travels across the country. We find copies in Ulan Bator and Tsibilisi – this literature gets the world's lowest circulation figures, but the world's largest reading circuit.

George spoke English with American accent and almost no Russian interference. He knew that I collected languages and words, so this lecture came as a bonus.

Entire books have been released like this. Valerij Tarsis was a rising star, had stuff accepted in *Literaturnaja Gazeta* and his novel *The Blue Fly* was partially released. *Partial* means that the *nomenclatura* did not bother to stop it, they simply did not understand it. Just as they did not understand Bulgakov until it was too late or Solshenitzyn, but as the book *A Day in the Life of Ivan Denisovitsh* sold extremely well they realized that here was something they did not fathom, they decommissioned both the book and the author and for many years he was held in custody in the Serbskij Institute, a psychiatric clinic, in many ways better than Lubjanka, the dreaded prison. You know, where you are heading …

Utter friendly our George, stout and ruddy, sucking on his right mustache. Cognac today.

– I mean, for you the easiest thing would be prison, it may be easy to be released from, in a way …

I was damn interested in this "in a way..." but eventually it would neither be Moscow nor imprisonment.

– And where is the samizdat fitting in, continued George.

– By mysterious ways one could smuggle out small handwritten pieces of paper, they were published gradually, and finally you have one entire book, *Ward 7*. In Norway you can just go to the bookstore and buy it.

And just that fact was Tarshish's life insurance. The psychiatrists suddenly found that he could not be cured, so they let him out, but the KGB, the Committee, or the citizen's committee as George contemptuously referred to the *kamitet gozurdazvennji,* they thought it went a bit too well for Valery so they turned up on his door–step, he opens door, sees who's there, tearing his shirt open with huge arm movements – he was almost 2 meters high – and roars:

– Shoot me! Shoot me, you can kill me, but you cannot kill the truth!

– This was also published in *samizdat*, says George.

– Many of the writers have a good imagination. But the real fun is served on *Radio Erevan*.

From what he told me, I realized it was a fictional radio station like KBBL–FM or Radio Free Roscoe, where they communicated frantic messages mocking the Party and all its assets in a tone of universal derision. Especially *aparatsjiks*, ambitious but totally loco local party bosses. George was particularly fond of the message of how they were achieving production targets for a nail factory, or was it light bulb factory? that failed to meet its goal of units produced per year. The factory then measured the output in watts, or inches as appropriate, and ...

– That year, you could only buy100 watt bulbs in the Murmansk district! Or 10–inch nails.

When a Russian laughs you might want to keep a distance ....

But the laughter is spicing our virtual strolls. As we "walked" in the Arbat, we visited a *Grusinian* (Georgian) restaurant I should visit later on – out of convenience, but also out of necessity. And always running underneath us – the Moscow Subway, the world's most beautiful metro.

And I colored the tales. With stories from the novels I had read; Gogol, Tshecov, books full of confused princes and officials on the brink of insanity from hunger and humiliation, and he laughed and said that in today's reality, it was mandatory that I bought myself a fur cap. Preferably black bunny, but typical Russian and not sticking out in any way, blending in, not in any way a head turner.

That was my first direct order: Buy a fur cap. And when we finally reached Moscow and entered the Hotel Astoria I immediately strode across the Red Square and into the *beriosh'ka* (toll–free gift shops solely for the benefit of tourists – and *aparatsjiks*) at hotel Russia, having the best selection. And I did not wonder why I already knew the way.

Beneath my freshly purchased black fur cap, my project is slowly growing and assuming its form: A young Danish bookseller and I will smuggle leaflets across the border, we'll distribute them at an appropriate place and time. If the planners had calculated correctly, we would not be automatically expelled this time, "because something will happen elsewhere that you do not have to worry about."

Well.

Then prison and despair will follow, litigation with the Western press ringside, in the streets the Russian masses will rise and Brezhnev and Kosygin – see how they run .... One stone face less in the world!

At this point we threw like a glass or two at the wall. George is almost done with me, we meet time and again for spiritual replenishment, but now Michael is waiting. The next leg takes place in Copenhagen, but first I'll have to find Michael in Malmö. Completely on my own I must find Michael.

But first I needed to know about the *NTS*. We demonstrated in the name of a group called *SMOG*, the initials of some libertarian group in Russian. And I have not forgotten what group. I simply and deliberately have actively suppressed the knowledge. Because it was a movement that did not exist, because SMOG was a sham and smokes screen that would sell us to the West. We were fishing in the waters where the troubled youth was marching in all directions; today the United States was the main enemy, it was the junta in Greece and no one really got shot in Prague? Disgust with the Soviet never reached beyond the rhetorical level.

So in between the ANC and the Viet Cong there was a place for SMOG. Which was exactly what the name said it was: a smoke screen. We were agents for the NTS. Little did we know about this mysterious organization, but the answer to the obvious question: Why didn't we just as well demonstrate on behalf of the NTS? was rather abrupt:

– Then you will be shot.

That seemed awful inevitable, so I dropped the subject. Anyway, we should demonstrate in support of two named people:

– *Svaboda Grigarjenka i Galanskov!* Free Grigorenko and Galanskov!

George tries to pretend he is a rebellious student, he is forever a farmer by his looks and that fact must have saved him from a lot, I believe. But he is personating me, the representative of SMOG spreading leaflets to the people, George was somewhat tipsy for once and has climbed the sofa, he is throwing a couple of old tram tickets all over the people being me and suddenly I realize that he envies me. Deeply and intensively he envies me – my youth, my unfettered–ness, my un–corrupted empathy, and my being able to visit *Mother Rossija*, I can just go there and wallow in all her charms and he roars one more time:

– *Svaboda July Galanskov!*

Almost intolerable, but I have to ask – I beg your pardon, but who are those two gentlemen? And I know that the author July Galanskov publicly took the authors and outcasts Yori Daniel and Andrej Sinyavskij in defense, and also believed that the patriotic author Boris Pasternak ought to be published in the Soviet Union and that was not quite appropriate. He was put in a penal camp but would actually be released, because of the demonstration I was to conduct. Thus it can be claimed that the demands I presented to the Soviet authorities actually were met. But Galanskov later was internally exiled.

Pyotr Grigorenko was a colorful guy. He was a general and one of Stalin's most decorated soldiers. Unfortunately for those in power, he was also a Tartar from Crimea, and he never forgot that Stalin happened to deport the entire Tartar nation before the war. From his position at the Frunze Military Academy this guy now quite frankly demanded freedom, independence and the right of land for his people. And the most abusive of all: He used the Soviet constitution as the basis for his claims. His only tactical mistake was that he demonstrated twenty-five years, too, early.

You can lock up the entire ethnic group, incriminate all intellectuals, crush, kill and destroy, but you cannot stop a Grigorenko. A nuisance. A twisted mind: for he will not be silenced.

And this beam of opposition was in need of Western assistance? Of my humble gesture from individuals abroad? Yes, because the general himself had proposed the slogan:

– *Mir i drusjba!* Peace and friendship.

But *Mir* also means *time*, and now it was about time to find Michael.

4

A SPY IN THE MAKING

– No, never... not in a hundred million years there is no way I am playing this foolish boy scout–game on the streets here!

They would teach me some chapters from the life of a spy and I felt strongly uncomfortable. Ever since I was a kid, I abhorred party games for older people to run around with a blindfold putting donkey tails everywhere with the utmost frivolity. It is probably a ritual that I do not understand. As a recent participant in political life, I had also evacuated when the campfire got blazing and incredibly poor songs were to be sung. Pathos and patriotism are hidden in the stoutest of robes, apparently.

George wanted me to play spy.

Not very dramatic stuff, but things like revealing if I was followed on the street, how the *mailboxes* operated, checking the monitoring of rooms, how to communicate during estimated interception, etc., and for me this was just a bit too much *Hardy boys*. And I had not even read those books.

George made me understand that from after landing on Soviet soil and up to the demonstration, I was totally on my own. So was for that matter also my Danish companion, but I would carry the leaflets. Day and night I'd carry the leaflets, and if I was caught and arrested before the demonstration nobody could help me. Then they could put me away for a year or two in a less pleasant camp for drug possession, or the like. My only protection was the overt political demonstration. So for a whole week over there, I was totally on my own. But one week became two weeks.

– You must learn to watch your back, said George.

But my objections were compact, I blushed all over and George shrugged and thought campfire thoughts, as it goes. He knew that I knew that one could not address the leaders in the Kremlin as if they were sensible people. This whole scheme was pure nonsense, it was like wandering about with a blindfold fencing with the donkey's ass! So he gave up, sent me over to Mike with the following laconic message for me:

You will find him in Malmö. Or he finds you. Although, you do not know each other it is mere hide and seek.

The Russian roulette was spinning. However, in concrete terms I would leave the Copenhagen train in Hälsingborg and embark a local train to Malmo. Where I should buy a map, go to a particular mall and get a newspaper and some postcards, they should be filled out in this way and that manner and should be posted in a certain mailbox that I had just found and then backing in my own steps to the train station where I would meet Michael and this was just about enough James Bond for me. But I had gathered that I needed some protection and my protection was my own caution. And what if it all went really wrong?

– Use your head! George said.

Full of comfort.

So I disembarked the train in Hälsingborg and continued by a local line to Malmo. I glanced at the watch and noticed that in about three and a half hours I would meet with this Michael. And discovered that I would give myself away immediately if I just bought that map of Malmo. I figured that I *should* be found, they wanted to show me how easy it was to target that suspect Mr. Gjengset – see how they run! So I went straight ahead in order to not buy a map.

But a newspaper and a coffee I bought, and thought about life at sea. I had never been to Malmö, which was a big enough city to maneuver in. I had been around, so Malmo was not a random city I did not know. A good city for *framing me* – a lingvical bastard between the phrase 'frame up' and the Russian equivalent: A trap must be set, there are traps everywhere I walk and they all collapse.

But after coffee, I feel quite fit. I got the tourist map in Oslo, memorized the necessary route at the train and now I have a reasonable time to buy a map of Copenhagen in a kiosk near the St. Petri Church in the old town. I shudder a little when it dawns on me that even in Malmo, they do have Peter and Paul churches, just as in Leningrad. But I won't get so far. Just Moscow for me, if you please. Little did I know ... I shook off that sudden discomfort, as easily as I am shaking off my great persecutor, wherever he is out there.

In a leisurely pace I make my round, feeding some ducks swimming in a pond in Pildamms center, write my cards in a cafe in John Ericsson street, find myself a mailbox and keep on strolling back to the Central Station where a puny little middle–aged gentleman asks me if I speak English and whether I know if the boats for Copenhagen do leave from the east or west harbor area and I am about to respond as the sweat starts coming out of everywhere and I realize that I'm going to be shot here and now.

He laughs his impeccable little laughter in the midst of his impeccable suit somewhere and warmly presses both my hands, he has just applied our agreed–upon key words, about the ferries to Denmark, and I am hopelessly exposed.

But Michael is his name and is very happy. Now he knows that I know that this business isn't exactly party games, and Michael is quickly turned into Mike. Thin and puny, careful dresser and a magician with pots and pans. Take a walk in the park for him means hunting for lurid mushrooms I've never heard of, chestnuts or nuts of some clandestine order and I am a little nervous that one day he returns with a squirrel. He looks at them with a hungry look, and I will not at all mention the ducks in the pond!

Mike is a survivor. He is about to teach me "to disappear myself." Via Russian such a linguistic impossibility will be possible in English. But he had found me without any effort. Quite embarrassed, although I had tried to watch my back pretty good, stopping now and then, looking into the windows of the shops, resting a bit on a bench and no one had followed me?

– Exactly, says Mike.

– No one followed you. Listen up. The KGB are not idiots, though many of us represent them that way. I did not follow you, I "followed" you in front of you.

He told me that if one has to watch one's back, there are mirrors everywhere: the finish of the car's surfaces, the glasses worn by oncoming people, doors that open up, your own shoes and this is really too easy. Once one knows who to keep an eye on, it is actually better to follow them up front, any persecuted person do look over their shoulders. It was Mike's job to teach me. But how did he know who I was?

– Simple. You took a cigarette from a pack of ten Teddy's. Only available in Norway. A blend almost solely smoked in defiance by young intellectuals of right–wing inclination, not far from the environments of the so–called anthroposophists, from the teachings of Rudolf Steiner. I blushed some more and gave in unconditionally, from now on totally in Michael's custody. Absolutely necessary in order to avoid unwanted custody before due time. He sensed my embarrassment and fetched a piece of cake for both of us.

– You have wonderful cakes here in Scandinavia. He sucked delightfully on a spoonful of whipped cream and raspberry jam.

– Personally, I prefer the Georgine cake. The one they have in café Uncle Adam is among the best in the entire western hemisphere, the brittle bottom of brittle …

It dawned on me that we had been sitting in the same café when I wrote those postcards.

– Which means that … I was sitting exactly where you also …

– You must learn how to look at people. Or look at people without looking at people, more precisely. You must learn to notice what you do not know that you see. But it is a matter of training. Much like learning to remember your dreams, more or less. But the Georgine cake is almost worth a trip, so I have all my meetings in Malmö, if possible.

I lost interest in my piece of cake, I'll learn how to "disappear me" in a world that does not exist, says George – *njeta problema* but funnier in English: *piece of cake* ... And in the middle of a cream–filled piece of cake Mike predicts that I am going to starve in the Soviet Union.

– Hunger strike. The fat disappears and the pressure increases, smiles the well–dressed gentleman.

He has starved. I can see that now. Once he has been starving and it was not the least bit enjoyable, and as it is with some who have experienced starvation: He can no longer put on weight. The innermost cells of his body have learned a lesson, they throw themselves eagerly over the tiniest calorie and exploits it down to the smallest shred so not a milligram is wasted. And with some cream on the spoon he demands the same of me.

Well.

But then I need something in return. I would like to learn something about this sneaky NTS, the organization I am supposed to represent – this mysterious employer lurking deep in the myths somewhere. I tell him that George probably does not live in Munich as he claims but rather in Frankfurt, where there is an obscure little exiled Russian publishing house called *Possev* and ...

– Am Main, Mike stopped me.

– Frankfurt am Main. That's right. He sighs.

– The less you know, the less you can confess. He looks at his watch and utters that we need to make the hydrofoil for Copenhagen, but my persistently nagging has apparently worked. He gives me NTS:

– The National Alliance of Russian Solidarists.

– You are saying...

– In Russian: *Nacional'no Trudovoj Sojuz* (Национально Трудовой Союз). Mike gave me a piece of paper, just a copy from a typewriter with traces of carbon paper that read:

"Unlike Communism, Solidarism provides a twentieth–century basis for dealing with present day issues. It rejects a purely materialistic approach to social, economic and political problems. It postulates that man, rather than matter, is the chief problem today. It rejects the concept of class warfare and hatred, and seeks to replace this dubious principle with the idea of co–operation (solidarity), brotherhood, Christian tolerance and charity. Solidarism believes in the innate dignity of the individual and seeks to safeguard as inalienable rights his freedom of speech, conscience and political organization. Solidarists in no way claim that their ideas represent the final answer to all problems, but they believe that man who is master of the atom bomb must also become master of himself and his destiny."

Not at all far–fetched, but somewhat weird in the aftermath of 1968.

– This was agreed upon in 1967, said Mike – as if he were reading my thoughts. – George will fill you in.

At our last meeting in Trondheim, I get a story of George, the story of Vlassov.

– General Andrei Andrejevitsj Vlassov had miraculously survived Vissarianovitsj' (as far as I remember he never mentioned Stalin's name) officer–purges, but was taken prisoner by the Germans in 1942. He was a strategic genius, and perhaps Jossip (again Stalin) was aware of this, at least the German general staff realized that rather quickly. He was put in charge of two divisions of Russian prisoners of war; he became head of a sort of "Russian national committee", and set to manage a defeated Russia on behalf of the Germans, so to speak. But Vlassov was a cunning fellow and had his own plans: With German help he would crush Joseph, then he would convince the bulk of the Red Army who all were Russians more than Soviet citizens, to side with his army and then throw out the Germans. A brilliant plan! But Hitler was even more calculating. He must have suspected something, for Vlassovs divisions were spread throughout the German front, and Vlassov lost the unifying overview and the necessary command.

– Still he followed his intentions. Certainly they did not overtake the Man of Steel (*Stalin* means steel), but Vlassov joined the Allies in Prague in 1945.

George is raising his drink with alarming frequency at this point in the story, and is forgetting to suck his mustache.

– He was captured by the Americans there. Stalin (*tada!*) had developed a personal hatred of Vlassov. It was unquenchable. Before anything else would happen at all, he would get Andrei Andrejevitsj. No Yalta without Vlassov! While Stalin quietly detained all the soldiers who had been German prisoners of war, he played five–card with the warlords with Vlassov as the main input.

New sip in a cloud of smoke. George smokes Pall Mall incessantly.

– The Americans gave way. They surrendered Vlassov. Long silence.

– The rest is history. It is told that Vlassov was hanged. But he was hung on a meat hook and transported slowly through the Moscow boulevards, he lasted a long time where he dangled like a live but slowly dying symbol of treachery.

New long silence. Mustache sucking.

– He became a symbol for us, I mean Vlassov. He became the movement's symbol: First off with the bandits in the Kremlin, then out with the invaders.

And here was a covert Pan–Slavic program that I should have been far more responsive to. I had gotten a glimpse of the soul of the NTS.

But now Malmö. Filled with new knowledge about conspiracy Georgine–cakes, we enter the hydrofoil bound for Copenhagen, spiralling to new meetings and pure rock and roll.

5

THE BRAVE TIN SOLDIER

Foil in full speed over the ocean.

Copenhagen slowly growing into shapes of a city through the haze, it is December and cold and tepid winds are fighting for command over the lower layers of air but the tower at Kastrup rises above the mist and insists that here is a huge city. The contours of a warehouse materialize and two ships from Maersk and cranes from Burmeister & Wein are becoming visible, just like the plans for my near future.

We, that would be young Axel the Dande and myself, should take part in a so–called theater trip. First, Moscow, the Bolshoi ballet, then Leningrad and the Kirov ballet. More ballet and opera than pure theater for obvious reasons, and Peter, our Danish ticket–master thinks we'll watch Evgeni Onegin. He was a bit puzzled when I asked about what was on, it was quite irrelevant he argued with blinking eyes, filled with idealism. For him, the Case was the prime issue, but I've never understood why you cannot enjoy the Case tastefully glazed. So still a little unsure he admits that yes, we've tickets for this and that, they were so far included, and I insisted on proper seats in the Kirov Ballet. Mike smiled in the background, he coughed so lightly that Peter understood all by himself how important it is that we make ourselves visible to the tour operator by for instance making complaints about tickets we have no intention of using.

It did not dawn on me until afterwards: I really did have wonderful tickets to a ballet I would never get to experience. But now, I needed some exercise. And because Axel was not coming until later that night – he was selling fountain pens in his own little shop on *Strøget*, the famous shopping street – Mike was instructing me about open and hidden mailboxes.

That game finally ended up behind Warhol's version of Campbell's soup cans at Louisiana, the permanent art exhibition on the outskirts of Copenhagen. The spy game was over. And now we should meet with Alex, getting to know each other and then plan for our career as street artists in Moscow. But Mike would reveal that in the restaurant, they had an excellent fish soup. However, it is not very good in Denmark because they have so much bottom fish, just skin and bones, but he suspects the manager for nicking some Norwegian cod and salmon, I could clearly imagine the chef rowing his tiny boat in the morning mist every day at six o'clock, the Oslo ferry growing as a mountain over him and suddenly one cod after another sailing down into his apron.

But he does not bother cleaning the prawns. Here you have to suck them clean yourself. Provides a taste of the ocean so you really have to check that you are ashore.

We are alone in the room. Mike were talking about something completely different. He does that a lot. Not a word of praise to be heard. About the training I have put down and the demonstration coming up. But as he says – piece of cake. He really was picking his words! He briefly outlined the plans, Axel had already been briefed. We were going to smuggle five hundred leaflets into the Soviet Union, it was most convenient to carry them in a custom-made belt around the waist.

We have got tickets for the Bolshoi Ballet on our last night in Moscow before traveling on to Leningrad, but Axel and I could possibly be somewhat late ... a year or two. When asked directly, Mike answered that a crime like ours would be rewarded with three to five years.

– But we must keep up the pressure! There are committees all over the West besieging the press, and moreover, we will put on something spectacular. That you certainly do not know anything about. It's for your own good. We will study the details later with Axel. You have first class tickets, but at half-time you enter the upper galleries on either side, you have eaten your belts and half of the *listos* (leaflets in Russian) each distributed on your four inner pockets, and just after the opening chords, let's say eight bars into the overture – you let loose the squall of snow! ... What a riot! Instantly you are heroes of *Rossia* and enemies of the Soviet Union, as long as it lasts.

He fell silent.

– I would have wanted to be there myself. You have no idea...

Long silence.

– Your job is to make sure you get that far. I think you can do it.

He finished his seafood, cleaned the plate with the last bit of garlic bread and proclaimed that during the weekend we were to practice communication and monitoring and such, and Axel and I had to solve each our puzzle, and find our meeting place no one knew where was. But Axel and I were pulling Mike's leg. We had agreed on meeting at the pub *Laurits the Valet*, we were both relaxed about this idealism thing and had learned the importance of providing just the right amount of give a damn, Axel gave me a book by Hans Jørgen Lembourn on the way home after the first session, the author was actually a dentist and elected for the national congress for the right wing party, but when the title read *Kick my traditions* I was helplessly lost.

Before the avalanche: The evenings in *Laurits the Valet*, in daytime roaming the terrain with the Woodchuck Manual in my hand. I went home to celebrate Christmas as if nothing would happen.

6

THE MYSTERIOUS
RESISTANCE

Axel filled the whole room all by himself.

– 'Morning, he says, so you are the man!

Axel is huge, tall and broad with a beard and glasses, and it's like no room for any extra abdominal belts on him. He is very happy with his body. After the meal we take measurements. I should wear an abdominal belt, which will be hand–made to our next and last meeting in January. We spoke about ways of communication. Axel and I did not know each other but we must get acquainted in a natural way. It might as well be the first night in Moscow when the group will be gathered in the bar for foreigners at the hotel. Not before. We must not know each other upon arrival in the USSR. His name was on the leaflets, and if I were stopped at the passport control, Axel would return to the plane again and seek protection from the flight crew. Therefore, we flew with SAS, although Aeroflot was cheaper.

This I thought sounded pretty dubious, and for the first time I began to doubt the intelligence that my own safety depended on. Walking out to the plane again if I was taken aside? I fantasized about a forest of Kalashnikovs, snarling dogs and impenetrable barbed wire. Or worse. Later it turned out that Axel harbored the same concern. One could measure the turbulence by the width of his grin and the cigar–sucking frequency. In Moscow, we were really SMOG.

It was entirely reasonable that any conversation of interest was taken outdoors. Inside, we were bugged everywhere, there was no point in aborting the microphones, but it could be fun to find them, and if we were exchanging messages when inside, they had to be written. Just some clues, and after use we had to tear the messages into pieces of paper so small that they could be flushed down the toilet, not burn to ashes in the ashtrays.

My mind was inevitably working on this matter with NTS: *Narodno–Trodovoj Soyuz*. I looked it up in my newly purchased phrase book and found *population–worker union*. This sounded very Soviet–ish, but I had also found that this people's and workers' union was regarded as enemy number one of the Soviet–state. And suddenly I was not so sure anymore: Was this a couple of numbers too large for all of us? KGB had enemies under every bed, and if we were running errands for the main enemy, they would come down on us real hard.

Christmas passed by. In the middle of January, I told everyone that I was going to Oslo and would be gone for a week or so, I had a fresh passport and had paid student's tuition fee. In Copenhagen, there was a mood of melancholy. We had studied the tickets like three hundred times, we had checked each other's luggage, abdominal belts were tested and adjusted and I was glad that the era of corset was over – but it wouldn't show if I kept the jacket buttoned. Not exactly the fashion of the time I protested, but they got me a double–breasted jacket and it was just too much even one for a young person from the upper middle class. Anyhow, the atmosphere was lackluster. George was there and taught us the three most important words in Russian: *basjalst, spasiba* and *nazderovja:* Here you go, thanks and toast! It would suffice in most situations. And a piece of advice, no champagne before lunch. One had to bear in mind that this is a country where the main question of the day is whether one should choose vodka or brandy for breakfast?

Ultimately all required words were said, and tomorrow Axel and I would not know each other.

7

BACK IN THE USSR

January 12th 1970, we landed at Tsjeremetjevo Airport outside Moscow. We squeaked through the cold air and over to a bus, soldiers with Kalashnikovs were posted everywhere. I was so far prepared for it: As a sailor in Leningrad five years ago, I saw them guarding the garbage barge off the ship. A crappy job. Here, after all, they had an airport to guard with dogs on a leash and barbed wire from tower to tower, we drove through the perfect backdrop for our worst expectations.

The cold was critical. But inside of me, it was pretty hot: Perhaps I would not experience much else of the Soviet Union than barbed wire and dogs on a leash. Capless and in trashy shoes I sweated uncontrollably and thought about all the good admonitions: Look effortless, don't let your eyes wander, think of something boring and I think of ... school.... in a country that might no longer exist .... And then giggling in sheer horror. I pulled myself together, glancing at my fellow passengers – here I wanted to look as little conspicuous as possible.

The belt is clutching. Like a soldier on guard, needing to stand perfectly still: Itching all over. Then I suddenly surfaced. The brakes of the bus screeched, coming to a full stop; a pair of plugs popping out of my ears and all of a sudden Soviet fell down over my head. Everyone around me are just as excited, we are heading directly into the Heart of Darkness and I'm not the only one with an itch. Suddenly I stop sweating, I'm the only one here who is prepared for the unspeakable, I think of beltless Axel walking into his immediate future full of fear and trepidation on behalf of me, here and now I'm his only life insurance and I will be a pillar of peace and am I not standing here yawning?

Some more steps forward in the cold, I spell my way through the sign *Tsjeremetjevo Aeroport* over the front doors we are passing through, gently in the background a memory of Churchill as I myself did not hear him in 1948: "An iron curtain has been drawn across Europe ... ". Again I feel the anxiety from the early fifties when we children with the bottomless gravity only children can muster, told our parents that we were afraid of a nuclear war and all the horrors and I am shaking powerfully inside my coat – this is pure madness. But the present was relentlessly knocking at the door: There is approximately one division trained soldiers between the terminal and the aircraft. The plan of an easy return to the plane for Axel if I was spotted, was pure fiction. Or worse: this was reality, no Copenhagen fantasies. The Iron Curtain was brutally torn away, there was no place for fantasies, and now there was ice everywhere and the Empire of Evil was here to be dealt with.

In the end I saw Axel up front with a fresh cigar and his fattest smile and for a moment I was reassured. It's almost brilliant to cover ones nervousness with a huge smile and suddenly I was sure that Axel could manage to smile himself right out of the Soviet Union if it should be necessary. He saw me and looked right through me, I was deadly impressed with all this professionalism and standing in line at the passport control was endurable. Later he told me that he remembered nothing from our little invasion, he was at least halfway into fainting.

Everyone was upset. No one could notice my anxiety, I was shaking uncontrollably and so did as Axel and a handful of others, stumbled onto a small bar they had found a space for out here just in front of the passport control and baggage delivery – where I bravely held on to a glass of vodka. The tremors gave way, the nerves were pushed back into place behind my skin. Slowly the four rows of tourists rocked through the passport control.

– Welcome to the Soviet Union! A female soldier smiled to me in English.

– And what is the purpose of your visit, she wanted to know.

– To demonstrate, I said. Making a hell of a noise and hullabaloo and worse! But really I was pretty dumb, sandpaper cramping the uvula and it was like that dream where you have to shout as loud as you can but cannot produce a single sound and everything falls apart around you because of the sounds you are unable to make and this insane desire to squeal, confess here and now it's all over in an instant so that you can sit there in your own deep hole with your head between your knees for the rest of your life, it's like riding slowly along a car and being drawn inexorably towards the side of the car and ...

– Theatre, I hear someone utter. I cough and hawk but there it was again:

– Theatre, we are here on a theater trip all together. Bolshoi and Kirov and ...

The soldier who looks like a woman smiles at me, and now she gives my name a try.

– Gi–jongset? Gonnar Chauk?

Not bad. My name is Hauk, impossible in a variety of languages and it was much worse the first time I met with a U.S. Immigration Officer. There, they expounded my name as Polish, *g* in front of *j* in English is impossible. The amended opinion when they came to my first name: Gunnar rapidly transformed into *Gunner*, plus *Hawk*, that made sense. But this was in New York. Here they were mighty pleased that I came all the way to watch theater, I laid out my keys and wallet and passport and such, and presto! I was inside.

The passport would be returned at the hotel, she insisted. Only partly true: they kept the passport pretty much throughout my entire stay. Then there was the luggage. Each one had to clear their belongings, just as at any airport. I glanced over my shoulder and noted happily that Axel was through. Now we were all set.

At the hotel, Axel and I had invested in single rooms. They were expensive, but necessary. One place you had to put off the assignment and breathe in and out all by yourself. I unhooked my belt and took a look at the room. Nothing strange, no visual appearance of microphones, a little disappointed I inspected the bathroom while the radio played patriotic music. The bathroom was patent. I took a shower, and in the background the patriotic music. I touched the belt had for the last time, tonight Axel was getting to know me and the pamphlets would be distributed among us and tomorrow morning I would be totally on my own in Moscow. And in the background the radio played patriotic ... hell! I rushed off to the unit to turn it off. I found a button and hit the applicant, the needle moving along the mysterious Russian names and I wondered if they received radio Luxembourg for example? Or Radio Free Europe or any other Western European stations? But all I heard was Russian, and noise and patriotic music and finally I turned it off.

That is to say, I tried to turn it off. It was not possible, I could mute the sound down to a whisper, but the radio did not turn off. Irritated I turned, and stood there with the knot in my hand. I had finally found the hidden microphone, or speaker, that worked both ways. Satisfied I poured myself a thimble of duty–free and dropped leisurely down in the easy chair with a highly appreciated western cigarette: the Soviet Union was thank God exactly what we wanted it to be.

Then I went outside, to experience the Moscow Nights. Now I really froze. The Moscow River was frozen over, ice lay with ten good inches on top of the sidewalks so one had to adjust the stride each time one crossed the street. Everywhere a whiff of cabbage and gasoline.

Now the belt is itching again, what will happen in a few days when we're standing there at the top of the gallery, throwing our propaganda from above – perhaps people will be pissed off? They seem well nourished and satisfied, perhaps they are proud of their system, maybe nine out of ten Russians truly believe in Breshnev and can one really trust these dissidents? And do really exiled Russians fully know what is happening in Russia, those who claim that the regime is ready to drop and just need a sharp blow to as crack as trolls do? Highly doubtful I slunk towards the hotel.

8

BREAKFAST OF CHAMPIONS

Breakfast.

A rather sumptuous thing in the Russian way, I think after a while. The waitress asked me how I wanted the eggs and I answer fried, thank you, and thus she comes with fried eggs – two.

– But I only need one, I objected.

She looks confused. But she soon finds her composure:

– We only serve two eggs here. But you may well get four?

And alongside the two lies a neat pile of bacon and some small sausages and fried potatoes and if I want chops? But this is more than enough and then comes the question of drink. I have been warned against Russian milk, and she asks:

– What do you want to drink? Vodka or cognac? Fifty or hundred grams?

And besides the funny fact that the booze is measured in grams here – as if one regarded drinks as something to eat rather than, well, drink – I noticed all those small flasks being carried around and found that this day could prove to become a very happy one, but I have a job to do and so I ask for mineral water. And yogurt. And coffee by no means, but tea, which is a huge disappointment: Lipton tea–bag, without lemon.

Axel was sitting over there. We had been properly introduced the night before in the hotel's bar and *berioshka*, the special shop strictly for foreigners. As was the bar. We had been introduced by the Danish travel guide Jytte to each other, but also to a couple of nice Danish ladies, Margaret and Hanne. The former two had a crush on Axel, and today Jytte is sullen but Margaret is happy and Hanne is sharing table with a Russian. I decide to keep far away from her, she smells conspiracy. Axel and I stroll up to my room, where no events have taken place during the night. I point out the radio, he has experienced the same thing, we turn up the patriotic music and talk loosely about today's program.

– Are you in for a tour of the Kremlin?

I confirm that I wanted to take part, so I could learn a bit about the Tzarina Katharina's hideous horse–drawn vehicle with eight boggies and sixteen wheels plated with gold and the suspension so rigid that they needed the total width of the Red Square to turn the monster...or the Easter eggs designed by Fabergè ... Axel says that he will see if he can find the Bolshoi Theatre and that is my clue:

– But we haven't got tickets there. The Bolshoi is occupied by the Paris ballet corpse and what are we going to see instead?

Innocent question, serious crisis. The leg–work of our SMOG–mates had been too lousy: This ballet–swop had been known in the Russian press for a long time and it would have been impossible to get tickets to the Bolshoi for several months if you did not have contacts high up in the *nomenklatura* somewhere and none felt for calling Breshnev. Whereupon Axel mimed that he would make a call, we brought with us names of people to call, Western contacts that would inform the Western press about the time and place of action. This was our life insurance: Without witnesses, no reports in the Western press and thus no Western pressure on the Soviet authorities. In that case, the demonstration would be dangerous for us. We did have an emergency number, and now we had a crisis building up.

But today's program was fixed: Axel should check press contacts, see if there were any tickets in the black marked, when I were in the Kremlin. From slowly spelling our way through the headlines, we had gathered that the Bolshoi Ballet was temporarily moved to the Congress

Palace, it was where Breshnev usually is giving his four hours speaches from time to time and I really wondered how that drunkard and chain smoker could keep going on for four hours? Maybe he did the Lenin stunt – wax doll on stage. Breshnev was usually as vivid as the wax doll in the Lenin mausoleum.

But first I should get rid of the belt. We had free time until lunch; with the Red Army Choir on the radio, we went enthusiastically at work. We talked constantly about the most absurd things, two silent men in the room was very suspicious. So I sing *The man is 'after the beer* and it is obviously a well–known Danish glee–song and we both sing our lungs out, it goes well with the belt we are going to eat.

We have disfigured the belt. We have dismantled it completely and totally, with his little scout's knife Axel had cut it into small stripes, we wrapped them into several small paper packages. But we lacked paper, and so did Russia as well – paper of any sort was a scarce commodity. So Axel had been to the nearest grocery store yesterday evening and bought two bottles of champagne and some beer. A weird experience. They wrapped the champagne neatly into the tissue paper but grew angry when he let the lady know that he would like to have the beer bottles wrapped as well. He got a lecture about cheap beer and precious paper, stuck the bottles in his pockets and padded back to the hotel. He pointed to his head:

– The Russians are crazy!

We distributed the small packages discreetly inside the clothes, we have divided the five hundred leaflets into two piles and they fit precisely into the inner pockets of a dinner jacket. It's showtime!

But first: After lunch there are laxatives and the corpse of Lenin. Some from the company appears to have digested too much of the liquids but rather sparsely of the food. Which was fried fish, whitefish and char and other sweetwater fish that I do not know the name of, Axel settled down at the table and looked absolutely inappropriate.

– I'm certainly not feeling too well. My stomach is unkind, it's all that fatty food ...

Kremlin was sumptuous. Not the least difficult to understand the necessity of revolution, having seen such a collection of insane wealth.

– But was it really necessary to assassinate the entire Tsar family because of that? an elderly Danish woman asked, she vividly imagined herself in some of Anastasia's opulent dresses.

Myself I was here to see the Congress Palace. Known from TV, almost no level difference between the audience and the podium and totally unsuitable for our demonstration. Set in a new building of glass and steel among the Kremlin domes and totally misplaced. I considered the gallery, but on a trial round afterwards I discovered that all the visitors there were thoroughly checked. Not odd at all, the Soviet leaders were at large on stage and they were terrified by the recent shots in the United States, killing off two Kennedys and one Martin Luther King. Among others. It made reason, according to George and Mike.

The Congress Building was held in modern Western style. Out in the halls, there were plenty of pay phones, I tried two of our bankers but the number lead to a Russian anwering machine. Axel experienced the same, he told me later. We were thus not able to reach our press contacts, and for us to call telephone information would be very risky. We could not ask for help, because we could not reveal any names – and our call would seem somewhat suspect. We could only use an agreed code that only contained the date, and if anything went wrong we should contact an emergency number: A mysterious Russian who had a different code. But even here – no response.

The entire telephone system throughout Moscow had been given a total makeover. They had introduced the area code as was the case for the rest of Europe. But our foot soldiers should have known about it! Had I found out about the pickle this ignorance had left us in, I would have aborted the demonstration.

But this I knew nothing about. We were coaxed into the queue to the Lenin mausoleum, and inside the mausoleum, in front of a wax puppet of Vladimir Ilyich Uljanov who had family in Vadso, a city close to the Soviet border; his brother was skipper on a fishing boat in the Murmansk region and lived well on the Pomor trade between Russians and Norwegian, first and foremost run by the Samis. But this deal was quite suddenly brought to an end in January 1918, and brother Uljanov did not return from his last deliverance in the Varanger fjord, he married and settled in Vadso and started the Uljanov family, as he still called himself.

Just entertaining myself while queueing up to have a look at a corpse. Unbelieveable! Kilometers of Soviet citizens queuing up for a bloody corpse ... and not even bloody. But inside of me, this gnawing uncertainty. Axel seemed ill when he entered my room.

– I think I have a serious stomach problem. It has bothered me before, but now it is directly painful. Maybe I do not want to take part in the whole tour.

– But can we go for a little walk? I passed a small pharmacy, there were at least some mortars on display in the window.

So we went for a walk, mostly to be able to talk undisturbed. Axel was still determined to take action, he thought the food and drink and anxiety and tension caused disorder signals in the food line, he agreed that charcoal tablets might help, and I had actually seen a pharmacy–like shop just down the street. We found it but did not know what *coal* was in Russian, steel was the same word as Stalin, *man of steel.*

– *I am looking over Stalin's head and out*, Axel recited.

– Excuse me?

I had just told Alex about my meeting with Lenin, it was George who had commented that the mausoleum had been plagued by floods twice and that therefore it was inconceivable that the remains of Lenin and other revolutionary heroes were still intact. I could see for myself that Stalin was gone, Lenin himself tried to get rid of him as early as 1925, but the Man of Steel survived and lived on in Western myths, until the Finnish poet Pentti Saarikoski wrote the collection *I am looking over Stalin's head and out.*

– Many who stayed with Stalin, said Axel.

– But think of Majakovski, the Russian Revolution's great poet Vladimir Vladimirovitsj Majakovskij, he wrote a poem that filled an entire book called just *Vladimir Ilsjitsj Lenin*, "From this banner, from every fold, the living Lenin still is calling: Workers, we march to the last battle!" And then Lenin dies, and then Majakovskij shoots himself.

Axel confesses that he not only sells fountain pens, he's also a bookseller. And now he has met an interesting elderly gentleman, a member of our expedition, his name is Johannes, and they've had a conversation about Danish poetry and modernism.

– I have invited him to dinner tomorrow evening, I have mentioned you and it will be just the four of us. Then we'll make up something. I have an idea …

– Four. You surely need an abacus…

We were deeply impressed by this toy-like item the attendants quickly manipulated with alarming accuracy in every shop and at every counter, they would have beaten a cash register with flying colours with any abacus.

– Margrethe is coming as well, of course. We spend some time together, you know, but as yet, I have not told her anything. That makes four.

I did not approve of this development. If she fancied Axel, she might not be delighted over his action and possible detention. Lesser news can trigger stomach problems.

Axel explained the way to the Bolshoi Theatre, on top of Gorky street. I had an errand in the Gorky Park the next morning, there was a safe mailbox for weary agents. I found the park without problems, I had noticed the actual stop on the metro. Funny how the big boys here changed their names for Lenin or Stalin or whatever. Gorky's real name was Pesjkov. And what was so wrong about that? A practice I do not quite understand. But here in Gorky's park someone had rigged an ingenious mailbox. That is, it was really quite easy. On a bench just inside the eastern gateway I was to sit down. Then one would spot a small pier into an artificial pond, the water was heated so the pond never froze over, the water was allways around plus two degrees Celsius.

There was a small boathouse there, and beyond a section of lockers where swimmers could drop off their clothes, and a tiny cupboard for watches and wallets for those who just tore off their clothes for a quick dip. I had the keys for locker number 10. There were no people there at this time. Good: I was followed and good: I did not have to go for a swim. It would have looked suspicious to lock oneself into one without diving into the icy water.

No message. Our contacts had not heard from us, but they had not found it necessary to leave any new instructions. This could mean that they thought everything was on schedule, or that they knew that it was not but could not act freely, or that their group simply was blown. I left the agreed message there: A postcard showing the Kremlin. The meaning being: *make contact.* We never heard anything.

Axel and I were all alone.

9

...THEN EVERYTHING WENT HORRIBLY WRONG

– We need witnesses, concluded Axel after having informed me about his idea.

The conversation slowed down a bit, we were all hungry and Axel had several meals to catch up with. Rather drowsy we got some coffee with the brandy, and Axel leaned across the table:

– We need some help.

And he talked about what he had in mind: We were about to launch a demonstration against Breshnev, by distributing leaflets claiming the freeing of the two dissidents Galanskov and Grigorenko. The original plan was to demonstrate in the Bolshoi. That demonstration would not take place, we had to invent something new, and therefore we needed witnesses tomorrow night. We should find a suitable place, so if the two of them could just stand beside and watch, and then contact the major news agencies as soon as they landed at Kastrup. Our entire audiences kept very quiet.

– So what, then, here comes the real explanation for why we could not get tickets to the Bolshoi, Johannes said thoughtfully.

– We can blame it on you!

But he was not angry, just puzzled.

50

– You might not know what has happened today, here in Moscow. So far no one knows, for it has not really happened.

Axel and I knew nothing, our secret agents were apparently not capable of understanding our clear messages.

– Bolshoi Theatre is essentially closed to all foreigners, they just do not inform about it, they have been waiting for some kind of demonstration, there's been just a few over the past year, and the demonstration came but not in the Bolshoi. Western intelligence was better than the Sovietic!

Johannes smiled happily, perhaps that old rentier had smuggled ibles once and we did not find it neccessary to tell him what *we* had experienced of unreliable intelligence. He continued:

– The reason I know this is that I passed the TSUM mall today, the GUM is so unpleasant with massive security because of that demonstrating Norwegian some time ago, so consequently they chose TSUM, the second–largest mall in Moscow.

Of course! Simple, almost brilliant! Axel cursed and flushed, so TSUM, then, was also his idea. But a little too late. He already knew what Johannes was about to tell us:

– But complete chaos had happened upon that mall. Closed due to inventory, a poster read, but they were two young demonstrators, they were from the south, Italians one of the Russians in the crowd outside guessed, the atmosphere was nice and anti–Soviet.

And then everything went horribly wrong.

Johannes appeared quite excited, he was probably more anti–Soviet than he would admit and surely more than I. Anti–Soviet i did not know, but I was opposed to their very rude ways of governing. People did not disappear here, it was the system that disappeared people.

– Probably a boy and a girl. They had thrown leaflets from the upper gallery, they had cried *svaboda* (release) someone – and we actually knew their names for they appeared on our own flyers as well– but the rest of the message was quickly drowned. This time the police were prepared, they were removed immediately, the traffic outside was led through other streets and after half hour it was business as usual.

Not a word in the newspaper.

George had mentioned other spectacular actions and I wondered what insurance these protesters had, were Western media present, were they to engage in a hunger strike, or was the Soviet militia really so effective that they had strangled the whole demonstration? We were certainly in big trouble, Axel and I. Perhaps *our* action would serve as the Italians' insurance, were we to provide a focus for more action? I knew that the goods had to be delivered, in some way. So did Axel. After a grown–up brandy, he continued, the smile on widescreen and toffee in his voice:

– So everything is developing as expected. The only problem is that we were the ones to steal the show in the Bolshoi, and that will not happen, and we can not get in touch with our contacts.

Directly to Margrethe:

– We need someone to attended to the whole shabang, we can not write anything down but just remember that we will go on a hunger strike, you should talk to the one representing *Jyllandsposten,* he will hand you a completed, written statement, he is our man.

But his powerful speech made no response. Margrethe had been looking down for the whole last hour, and a friendly approach from Axel said she just barely answered:

– I really think you should consider your troubled stomach. After all, I am a nurse, so I cannot ...

With Johannes, it was even worse. He said a definite NO. And he had nothing to fear, he was old and could gladly put his life at stake. It was not that, but he was simply afraid that we would be rammed by the wrath of the Soviet leadership. If so, they would never budge.

– A political trial in the USSR is a serious issue nowadays. They regret bitterly the release of *A Day in Ivan Denisovitsj's life,* and it will not last long before Solshenitsyn's expulsion. It seems as if they are on the verge of taking the worst of chances for the time being. Just remember Bukovskij!

Johannes will not stop:

– I sympathize with what you intend to do. But you are so young! What do you really believe might happen to you? What's the worst case scenario? I want you to think about what's the worst that can happen, and then you go home and sleep right into the morning and when you wake up you will be certain that all will be for the worse.

Margrethe regarded him gratefully. Axel seemed relieved.

– Okay. So let's forget about it. You might be right.

He sensed that I got dismayed. But he gives me a heavy and soothing look: We'll talk about this tomorrow.

There is nothing much to talk about. We are walking in the Moscow night, it's quiet and peaceful and not as a Thursday evening in Oslo, no noisy gangs full of booze and hubris and the Russians are usually drunk in a completely different way than we are used to.

– Perhaps because they are drunk all the time, Johannes suggests. He invites us for a nightcap in his room, a night like this needs to be valued, he argues.

Last night in Moscow. Life appeared very different when we woke up, I saw military units everywhere and militia behind all the ornamental plants in the lobby. Maybe it was just my imagination, but it took oceans of time to get our passports at the reception. The others spoke loudly and enthusiastically about the Soviet state circus that they had visited the night before, I had hoped for tickets to the Moscow Art Theatre, Stanislavski's old scene. Hard to imagine how this beleaguered city was infected by a rush of liberties right after the revolution: Majakovskij rushing forward with his vast Lenin–poem, Skrjabin playing his mysterious pieces for piano, he invented an organ connected to a strobe–like canon pouring out beams of shifting light, projected directly on the skies over the Red Square and the botanist Valentijn Propp bidding the biologist Lysenko farewell, Propp always busy with language and folk–tales, Roman Jakobson weaving the first tiny threads in the linguical web that he would use his entire life to buckle up – on his eternal flight through Europe.

Suddenly it was over. People in the United States shoot their leaders, Soviet leaders shoot their people.

No chance for a demonstration in Moscow, the Italians had spoiled that opportunity. Plus the shortage of tickets for the Bolshoij Ballet. So, we had to continue to Leningrad, next port of call. Eventually, we were crammed into the bus on the way to the domestic part of Tsjeremetjevo Airport. We noticed no difference. Apart from no signs in foreign languages. Plus, admittedly, a simple buffet with lots of exciting Russian dishes, the Russian *babushka* with her huge *samovar*, here I finally got a decent cup of tea in the Russian manner. Yet the presence of police and soldiers was as massive as in the international section and I was terrified, of course. They were looking for us! Why this absurd security for domestic departures?

– Traveling in Russia is not a presupposition, Johannes explained.

– Not only is it not allowed to travel abroad, you have to have proper papers to go more than forty kilometers outside Moscow.

– You must be joking.

– Forty kilometers, my boy! The journalists here can tell you that you must apply for an intern passport in due time to cover sudden news taking place outside these forty kilometers. Impossible working conditions. Features must be planned years in advance.

– But so what?

I did not fully grasp the scope of this, which was that a foreigner could always travel around, but after careful consideration. The Russians could travel freely, but hardly at all.

There was a lot of queues, local inhabitants had to show off their travel documents, we foreigners had to show our passports and our students legitimating cards, our vaccination cards and military service books and birth certification cards and ...

I had to calm down Axel. It could not be that bad. It was far worse. Something had gone absolutely wrong, we thought. They had put the twist on the Italians and they had given us up, but did they have any informations to offer? We knew nothing and that's the worst there is.

We had to cope with the situation. How about the upcoming control? It was time for Russian roulette. We noticed that all foreigners were intimately checked, not everyone, but many. Otherwise it was a relatively simple control, the tickets were distributed at one desk and passports submitted at another, and they only checked that your picture fit. I had noted that they were particularly interested in my American endorsements, perhaps they sensed a fragrance of the CIA and the like; Norway, neighbors and NATO, a delicate balance that usually was to Norway's advantage. But why was I the sole Norwegian on a Danish theatre trip?

Therefore, Axel had to bring the leaflets into the aircraft. We went out to the toilet along different routes. We swapped coats. Axel put all the leaflets in the inner pocket of his coat. I got that coat. We carried both the coats over our arms. Most men present did that. It was hot in here, and we had been here a long time. Very long time. Approximately a month, I assumed. For this was even worse than the admission, we were totally unprepared for this and we just had to rely on the decency of Johannes and Margrethe if we where were hooked.

On a rather uneven row we should pass between two counters, it was all very open space, we really were *in* the Soviet Union all right and not on the way in or out. We discussed the plan in not so many words: Heading steadily for the buffet, eyes in the neck and ears on each finger. We left the restroom, Axel with my coat over his arm, I with his coat over my arm. The plan? Swapping coats.

– We have got tickets to the Kirov–ballet in Leningrad! Our guide Jytte cried triumphantly. And this was compensating for the Bolshoi, and I wondered how the gallery looked in this theater? I got my hopes up for a peaceful demonstration, both Johannes and Margaret would become witnesses much against their will, an absolutely excellent plan was slowly growing into shape and I saw that it dawned on Axel as well. Completely effortless and without the slightest difficulty, I ordered fifty grams of vodka.

It was time to head for the counters. Axel and I had our fragile plan. We had to stand side by side when approaching the counters. We would argue vehemently over a book I had brought out of my luggage completely at random and it was *My life* by Gorky, we hoped that they read Latin letters, and otherwise we should pronounce *Gorky* as often as we could, send the book back and forth between us and simultaneously juggle our gowns to confuse the poor guards.

A pure and simple magic show, in other words. The hand works quicker than the eye, but Axel was so nervous that he rose to rhetorical heights and attracted almost more attention than was healthy. But it seemed to work, he was waved through, he would go in front of me, bend down for his bag, both he and his bag had been cleared but not his coat, but he grabbed his coat lying on my bag within the same motion and walked quickly through. Over my bag lay my own coat, completely free of leaflets.

The world's lightest man stood ready for inspection, I was so light I was almost ready for takeoff, I had to take a hold on to the desk for a moment and some claimed it was vertigo. In fact I had a black–out for an imperceptible second, I opened my eyes and looked at my fellow travelers and discovered that the second didn't pass unnoticed. The clerk or whatever gave me a curious look, but absolutely fearless, I looked him straight in the eye:

– Too much vodka. *Vodka krjepkij.*

He laughed. He laughed heartily at this foreigner who had already learned the most important Russian words and waved me on. Easily and effortlessly I stumbled out of Moscow.

Steeplechase out of Moscow, speeding into Leningrad.

10

LAST MAN STANDING

Slowly Leningrad rose up from sea.

Here it rose from the marshland, one of the world's most beautiful cities, as if it has sucked its beauty from the thousands of human victims of the marshes, as if it has a patina of the millions died in wars and revolutions. A city of canals, more beautiful than Venice, prouder than Stockholm. Water runs through them all, perforated as they are of rivers and canals and Leningrad is situated on all the banks of the river Neva. And Neva is a delta with city wherever the ground it is dry enough, here are water routes to Moscow and the Baltic Sea and to the rest of the Baltic. And that is the Meaning of Life for Leningrad – waterways from Russia's interior to the rest of the world.

A noticeably lighter mood spread when we were met with gentler degrees and open faces and people who actually owned their own faces and wore them with a grace that allowed us to understand that here we live entirely voluntarily. Half of our parents we have buried in the marshes so we do not travel, we could go water skiing to Helsinki any day but here we are here we will stay, and nobody can make us move.

Not easily ruled people like that.

As the owners of Soviet had realized. At all costs they must keep this city, they can't just let the people grab Leningrad and walk away. So people here could do pretty much whatever they wanted. So I felt free to walk alone wherever I wanted, Westerners were not as conspicuous as domestic folks and we could easily be a Swede or a Finn and therefore a cousin in every way. And people in uniform did not mind even their own people.

We checked in at the Hotel Europe, a hotel I have never checked out of. I must have a staggering bill there. In all: I liked it here. Eventually, Axel got so ill that he did not notice my change of mood. I had simply forgotten the mission, stacked it behind a brain flap, in a place where it shrunk and became as small as a pea, so if I shook my head the whole thing would roll out of the ear and down on the street and away.

Good for me. For the same day another menace to the society was arrested, this time a Dutch and this time in Kiev. An advantage that we knew nothing. Here I sauntered happily ignorant in the jaws of a whole commonwealth, jaws ready to collapse at any moment; in my pockets I had material deserving a maximum of five years in Siberia, or worse, and my only consolation and support was a fellow whimpering with ulcer. It is that kind of stupidity that often is confused with boldness. The war–hater Norman Mailer has written about how he became a hero in the Second World War because he felt such a momentary loss of common sense and reason. During a siege of a hill he just stood up, walked up the hill, dropped a few grenades down into the grave and bang! he had entered and conquered the height all by himself. I entered the Leningrad all alone, or Leningrad took all of me.

It is a time for happiness, and it is a time for sense.

Axel tried to pinpoint the cursor in all this love.

– You have got the leaflets?

– We have already reached Monday, by Thursday we will be going home and I have been confined to the hotel room and my digestion on full strike and my health in tatters ...

I am unable to find a way out of this.

And we need an exit. Now.

Loud and clear: Now.

If only we had a glass of something. For there hadn't been any opportunities in this shameless cultural cream cake of Leningrad. But now it is now. Axel:

– I most definitely must go home.

– Go home? You cannot just go home and leave me ...

– You were pondering over it yourself.

– Yes, I know, we need a witness, but then I thought of someone else.

– Someone else? And who would that be?

He was obviously right. Margrethe and Johannes had said no thanks. Perhaps just as well.

– Listen. I just have to go right home. It is for the best. I have a hell of a stomach affliction, you only need to touch it with a finger, and I will jump right into the sky.

– Sorry I've been preoccupied with Leningrad, but you're probably right. You will break down, a couple of powerful Russian will take a look at you and you will confess to the most wonderful things.

– Right. What if I with my stomach just have to sign anything to get help, and the day after the worldwide press will convey we have confessed to be young naive students who are here sponsored by Western bogeymen and smack! said the mouse trap.

He had a point. An obvious point. Moreover, it was not so stupid. It just was smart and necessary: Because with Axel going home, the world press would know about the campaign and thus was my safety guaranteed. And: It was quite obvious that no one has followed me here in Leningrad. After all, I would have noticed it. Therefore, I could go unnoticed in and out of the hotel, looking for a suitable place for my demonstration.

– I'll find a suitable place in the morning, I said.

– Thank you, I needed that, he said.

– We will visit the theater tomorrow evening then? he said.

– We will, I said.

Stoutness always comes easy for me, that's why my nose is upwards.

And Wednesday was entirely dedicated to the reconnaissance. Piece of cake, really. It would have to be a central location with a lot of people around two in the afternoon, I did not have the nerves to wait until evening and any action in the Kirov Theatre was off the table, this was basically a matter of timing and the spy's eternal waiting is definitely not for me.

So it had to be the Nevski Prospekt. The definite public street. Round two o'clock in the afternoon it was pretty crowded here, and the flight to Kastrup had it's takeoff at that time as well. Several of the passengers had further connections, and I was not the first Norwegian sailor who had been left behind. Pretty soon I found the perfect place: The mall *Gostinji Dvor.* A department store of four floors, originally a small beach cottage from the age of the princes and best of all: On the outside, on the first floor, a gallery ran along the entire length of the facade facing the Nevski, and with staircases at each end. I went there to try it out a few times and found that the corner of the Nevsky Prospekt and the Perrinajo line was the most busy among the corners of Leningrad. I could just take a stand and throw out my truths, even the weather was pleasant but I would certainly not be standing there alone for long. Good.

Then there was the question of a cafe. Clearly one must have a cafe with the correct view, to sit in and wait. And such.

A modest cafe in the corner of the Nevsky Palace Hotel was the place. I managed to study the menu in the window and noted an exciting fish soup, still hadn't lost all my wits and senses and besides I had some money left and then I might as well use them so I didn't have to pay for my fare if they just threw me out. I thought. Pure common sense, in other words.

But still we had some preparations to be made this evening before visiting the theater, in utter silence in Axel's room, which was bigger than mine. This time they had found out that it was necessary to have a drain in the middle of a hardwood parquet floor, for your ears only we thought and tomorrow at two o'clock, it would finally be all set. So we went to the theater and applauded loudly.

11

SHOW TIME!

Wednesday 05:00 PM:

Axel and I were staying in Axel's room, we had music going full throttle in order to allay any important messages, but the job was set – we had to remove Axel's signature from the leaflets. We tried to cut them out, but then we got the problem with the removal of the trimmings. Burning them would summon an eager hotel employee with his sense of smell intact, and it was difficult to flush them down the toilet. They were too easily clogged, as it was not used to paper. A joke!

So we deleted Axel's name from the petition with a ballpoint pen, from every damn one of them. Use your head, George used to say. We used our fingers. I did nor appear very professional either, the retouching only partly covered Axel's signature. More scratching, more cramps. But this should suffice, Axel would be airborne and out of danger when they were distributed. We made one mistake, though, in all the stress one of those manipulated leaflets must have crawled underneath somewhere and was found by the cleaning ladies. To our praise: We flunked grossly, but they flunked even worse: They were not able to decipher the name of Axel instantly, so they could not hold back the aircraft. This emerged during the trial – terror and delight in the same second for the defendant.

Wednesday 07:00 PM:

To the theater, to the ballet. The Kirov Ballet is considered by many as better than the Bolshoi that is a bit prima donna, now ballet is not exactly my cup of tea, and tonight they might as well display Nutcrackers on stage. The rest of the evening was pure mimesis.

Wednesday 10:30 PM:

Johannes told us a cryptic story:
– It is from a little book I always carry with me and it goes like this:
(He had written it down, he would not reveal the source)

– *The youth succeeds in its folly.*
I do not seek the young fool,
the young fool seeks me.
If he asks two or three times, then it is plagiarism.
If he bothers me, I render no enlightenment.
Endurance is promoting.

– Think about It. So I bid you goodnight, and will we be seeing you in the morning?

I'll be damned! Suddenly I was wide–awake and present with all of me in Leningrad in January1970. I recognized the text. It was from the *I Ching*. I have the same Danish translation myself. It was very decently done. And the meaning is: I do not know what you intend to do in the morning, young man. But if you'll be a fool, so shut up as long as possible so we at least can get home and thereby give you a glorious trial. The verse was the number 4 in the oracle book and was called *youthful folly* or *immaturity*.

Wednesday 12:00 PM:

So we hit the sack, and this my last night before the prison was just like my first night out of prison, me and my calm did not find each other.

Thursday morning I got up and felt just as light–headed as one is after five sleepless nights. It is a kind of intoxication in itself, in the middle of a tooth brushing you just drift off and in one corner of the eye you catch glimpses of funny things you prefer not to see. A perfect day for dying, as goes the old Indian saying. But I take my time, my suitcase is packed and I checked the room thoroughly. The airport shuttle was due at 9 in the AM, but I had already left the scene.

Thursday 08:37 AM:

I walked out of Gostonjitse Evropejskaia probably for the last time in my life, and had decided to take a stroll towards Gostinji Dvor. Perhaps they had dismantled the entire building during the night and I just had to turn and run back for the bus but there were only a few blocks down and there bold Gostinnji Dvor was waving with its balustrades.

09:12 AM:

All were gathered in the bus. That is, almost everyone. But travel managers did what trip leaders do, they checked the room and that the passport was in the lobby and stared soberly at their watches and then Johannes proposed that I was with him yesterday evening, and he is as quick and clever guy and he has probably hooked up with a girl or three, and he knows where the consulate is!

Axel:

– Yes, and he speaks Russian quite fluently, he knows both *spasiba* and *nazderovja* and he will get far, that boy.

And Jytte and Hanne gave them grateful glances and they are on the road. At last.

09:46 AM:

The Norwegian could not restrain himself and cleverly sneaks around the corner and checks that the bus has gone. Completely unnoticed, of course.

09:47 AM:

The airport shuttle is advancing to the Pulkovo Airport, it is only 15 km away from downtown, the poor travel managers need to explain what has happened and fear that it meant a devilish spectacle. For those who create havoc know what this might mean, but travel managers do not: They just have a hunch. And intense telephone calls are taking place:

Another demonstrator might be at large in the *Sovietskum Sojuz* and now they are almost out of rooms for more of that kind in their prisons. Hanne and Jytte were dumbfounded, this is nothing to make such a fuss about, Leningrad is the Soviet Union's one and only real port and they must have hundreds of left behind sailors all the time?

But the Russians are sweet and gentle towards them, if another demonstration is what they fear then do not let the West get wind of it. So, they soothe the band of agents and we will take care of this, it is probably a misunderstanding, but we will want to help him home and send him to the airport in the taxi when we find him and

10:30 AM:

... and still another half hour until that poor cafe opens so I went to the Finlandia railway station over on the other side of the Neva. It was a new and beautiful terminal at the end of the railway tracks from Finland. Or towards Finland.

11:30 AM:

"Witnesses Stepanova and Koloptin that discovered the leaflets in one of the premises on Gostonjitse Evropejskaia proved (said) that they were very upset about the cynical content of the flyer." (Court documents. Case W/–121 February 9, 1970).

11:31 AM:

A quick phone call from the hotel KGB to the airport KGB: It *was* the worst that could happen. We have a fascist–pig on the run, ready to pounce down on our heroic people with his poisonous propaganda. But the best thing that could happen: THERE IS ONE MORE! Keep the airplane!

12:00 NOON:

"SAS–DK something bound for Kopengagen is ready for departure" as it goes in Russian, but the Russians will just keep the plane, only for a few minutes, and somewhere the cops were working hard to decipher the retouched name of Axel, the Danish crew is a little annoyed and want to know what the hell is going on, it is not their problem that the Norwegian is drunk and for them he might as well swim home but they must leave, the have a lot of passengers who will otherwise lose their connections to half of Europe but let us give these troubled but helpful Russians a quarter of an hour but then! and the helpful Russians know that time is up, they have no legal reasons to stall the aircraft and the cops are sweating and Alex?

Alex had no sweat left. He has no misgivings anymore, he is one big one. What the hell may have gone wrong now? Axel gave me about four and a half minute more.

Then he untied his arms and gratefully accepted the drink the airhostesses served to compensate for the unexpected waiting.

– Give me a double, as well, please!

12:46 PM:

I am quite unconcerned at the corner cafe Nevsky Palace or whatever it was called and *piece of cake* I think, and think of Mike. Oddly enough I'm not hungry. So I decide for something simple, I try *blinis,* a kind of Russian mixture between a pancake and a donut with smoked salmon and Russian caviar inside. Soft food, stiff price. I pay, noting that I still have left a few hundred in Norwegian bank notes – and getting ready.

12:47 PM:

SAS–DK something is finally bound for Kopengagen and the cops have sweated out the name of Axel, whining jeeps over the airstrip tarmac and full alarm in all the watchtowers but no, captain Madsen and his crew did take off. Totally *Die Hard*.

1:47 PM:

I take off from the cafe, consumed with fear and dread, unspeakable things can happen and I will hopelessly be in the middle of it all. All of the time. I gather sufficient courage and get a glimpse of Kirovskij Prospect and think of Kirov as I wander to the place. It gives me great comfort. Everything here is called Kirov. No wonder, he was adored by the people, became a member of the Central Committee in 1934, and in December the same year he was murdered. A clean contract job. And the curtain went up for the Moscow–process and soon the curtain went up for me.

Saken N1-121   9. februar 1970

Dom

I navnet av Den russiske föderative
sovjetiske sosialistiske republikk

Kujbisjev-bydelens folkerett
i byen Leningrad

formannen   Antiosjko Z. P.
settedommerne Averina J. M og Golu-
               beva M. J.
sekretær   Lebedeva G. V.
med deltakelse av aktor Perfiljeva V.
og forsvarer   Heifets S. A.

har tatt til behandling i åpen
rett i byen Leningrad
         9. februar 1970

Saken om tiltale av Gjengset Gunnar
född 10. mai 1946 i Trondheim, norsk
student i 3. studieår ved Universitetet

The case w/-12   9th of February 1970

VERDICT

In the name of the Russian Federal Sovietic Socialistic Republic

Kuybysjev bydels folkerett
i byen Leningrad

Foreman Antiosjko, L.P.
Associate judges Averina, I.M.
              Golubeva, M.I.
Secretary Lebedeva, G.V.

with the participation of prosecutor Perfiljeva, V.
and for the defence, Haifetz, S.A.

has presented for tratment in open court in the city of Leningrad

February 9th, 1970

The case is a charge against Gjengset Gunnar, born 10th of May 1946
in Trondheim, a student in the 3rd year at the University

Or down, that depends.

1:52 PM:

I am rounding the corner of Nevsky and Perinnajo. A good audience. A little small maybe, but sufficient and what chattering do I hear? It's your heart that rattles my boy, I'm strolling unconcerned–like up the stairs to the balustrade, noticing that it is available in my corner, where many are taking a smoke. Not at all a bad idea, perhaps a long time until the next smoke, as I smoke I nearly giggle about how *that* would have been the top of nonchalance, flyers in one hand, a cigarette in the other and *Mir drusjba* in my chest.

Then I'm ready.

I stick my gloves in my pocket, take out the flyers, Axel on a plane to Copenhagen, Gunnar with flyers to the abyss.

SHOWTIME!

12

PEACE AND FRIENDSHIP!

– MIR I DRUSJBA!

No other sound is heard. The world is empty and quiet. Just a tiny little man full of peace and friendship. And out of his hand a white swirl of leaves in slow flight to the ground.

– Mir i drusjba! (Peace and friendship!)

A little more subdued now, the cars emit their sounds and the world revolving slowly. I sling a small handful of the leaflets over the railing, there are people around me on the balustrade but they do nothing, just stop in wonder and curiosity. Down on the streets, I see that the notes reproduce, a hundred white faces and white hands breed with papers. But quietly, quietly. A tiny miracle on a day in the life, a little cough of protest reaching out to them and no one will be interrupting this moment. Quiet ...; no militia, no police are invited into this moment. And people accept, read the text, talking quietly among themselves and stand perfectly still. More arrives, but no crowds, no disturbance.

I see it all, and never in my life have I experienced a greater peace.

So the miracle of it all finds *me*.

Someone is tapping me on the shoulder. I turn half around and I am prepared to throw away the last flayers for here they are, The Power is here but certainly not – behind me, people have lined up nicely with lightning speed, the Russians have understood the situation, it is like when the housewives in Moscow hear some rumors of bread being spotted in a shop and the next second thousands are waiting in line in front of the store.

It's just me finding it hard to understand what is going on, until the lady in front of the queue kindly extends her hand, I stretch out a flyer, she accepts and curtseys with a tiny *spasiba*, then she walks on and the next person is ready.

Reality is back in place. Nicely, they have queued up below the one staircase, parading one after another by me, *spasiba*, walks on and down the other stairs, the next person comes, *spasiba*, I have not a single word for an answer because all my feelings got stuck in my throat and for those minutes, I can pay days and nights in prison.

Then it's all over.

The whole thing lasted only a few seconds, I think, but my watch said fourteen minutes. The fourteen most peaceful minutes of my life. I cried for peace and got friendship, they want all the best for me and peace be with you but now you just have to go home.

For there is nothing more. Leningrad strolling calmly on, the acid sea breeze kicks in from the Gulf of Finland and everything is as always. Have I misunderstood it all? Have Brezhnev smoked his last cigarette that night and handed over power to the people? Well, I better go home then. Just get to the consulate and say I'm sorry, I missed the boat home but *smack*! reality strikes again.

Two men in plainclothes are pushing me up against the corner. They are two very angry, older men with their party membership–booklet spinning freely, for that is what they are fanning under my nose, indignant. There are only the three of us up here now. No one wants to participate in this. I have made my statement, we are very grateful, but you have to collect the bill yourself.

There is another kind of locomotion out there now. Men stomping the stairs with heavy boots. Cars whining to a halt, shouting angry orders. Finally I'm overcome by too many militias. They have their orders, uniform is a good enough presentation, the man does not speak Russian, however, and they lead me down the stairs, not by force but also not to be misunderstood. A whole cortege of police cars they had ordered for me. Numerous policemen teeming out of them, trying to disperse the crowd. And by now here is a real crowd, the young ones standing in front, they are standing there raising their clenched fists but not against me, they shake their fists against those who obstructed the view and rhythmically, I can hear it: *Mir in drusjba! Mir drusjba!*

Need I live any longer?

Another cut: swerving wheel around corners at a furious pace through the city, in haste to the nearest police station. Behind the counter, they push me into a chair and there they let me sit. There, they let me sit in peace, they know perfectly well who I am, they've got my business card and he has nowhere to go anyway. It is outside the counter it happens. Here they get shoveled inside, brutally, one after the other, young people who still have their voice intact and scowling the policemen and were thrown directly into jail. I recognize some faces from the crowd around me at the arrest and suddenly my moment is over.

The Moment of My Life has passed.

Maybe I'll suffer a little, but my suffering will be short. I have my governments to back me, I have Norway and NATO, and they only need to drive some tanks up along the border and I am free. But these young men are not freed. For them it will be prison and camp, but my moment is over, the rest is share embarrassment. Here are those who risk more than some minutes of their time. These were men of courage.

Parade for some, courage for others.

No one is talking to me and I sink into deep despair. This was only an acting, only a showing of ego and playing a guest role in The Real Existence and perhaps the only damage I have done was to satisfy my inner ambitions. Darkness at noon, until something completely unexpected happens: The situation has calmed down in the station, the officers have barely begun to swivel their chairs towards me, now it's your turn. Then three young people are coming up to the counter. Two men and a woman. They are quiet and polite, standing nicely lined up until it is their turn and what can I do you for? They explain what is the matter, it must be repeated, there is something incredibly about the inquiry, I'm following only partly until the spokesman delivers one of my leaflets to the police officer. I recognize Grigorenko with his general's cap. Now the other two do the same, suddenly there is a herd of uniforms around them and slowly it dawns on me.

They are giving themselves up to the police!

They reported to the police that look, we can prove that we participated in the illegal demonstration today outside Gostinji Dvor, and will you please be so kind as to arrest us, thank you very much! That's what happens. It is a matter of decency, I suddenly understand. It is not a matter of courage – courage is for mountain climbers. This is about decency.

An officer turns to me. I'm ready. He only says "wait here." I have no other plans, and pretty quickly here is a new uniform with a higher rank, as far as I can judge.

Hesitant English, but sufficient:

– We know who you are, Mr. Gjengset. We will offer you ticket to train tonight. You just sign this document, we keep you here some hours and simply drive you to the station, follow you to Finland, okay?

He pushes over a sheet for me. One of the worst things anyone can do to me is taking me for an idiot. The document is written in Russian, it would not have helped if it were in English or Norwegian, now I bring up the word I have been storing in wait for this situation:

– *Perivodsjik, basjalst!*

Interpreter. Roughly, *interpreter* is the correct translation. He certainly understands and therefore he knows he has lost, he is a likeable man in his early thirties, maybe he is directly benign, but he has his role to play:

– I strongly advice you two take this offer. This is nothing serious (he refers to the document), it only says I'm sorry for making disturbance, that you were mislead and that you will never again create disturbance in the Soviet Union. So please sign, for your own good.

– *Perivodsjik, basjalst!*

He goes one more round, he has his audience to consider, and this room is the quietest in the world right now.

– Please to sign. You are not an idiot (thank you very much!), so you must understand what that means. Prison, maybe for years, this is a serious offense, and you will be very lonely. Nobody in the West knows about this.

And without knowing it, or perhaps knowingly intentionally, he just told me about the commotion in the press and thousands of telegrams in all directions and Axel and Johannes –alive and kicking and now we are ready for the second act!

Smiling quietly now, and do I sense a relief there, a little secret glimpse of recognition? Maybe just dreaming, but still:

– *Perivodsjik, basjalst!*

He has nothing more to say, he is gathering his papers and rises, slightly taken aback by this opposition and waving to a couple of guys. He says something to them that indicates take him with you, find a suitable cell to heave him into it, then we'll see.

They found a suitable cell and heaved me into it, one turned to go but the other started towards me, clinging me to the wall completely consumed by rage, raised his fist and almost choking by his own cursing, I closed my eyes and waited for the white flash of a hit until he was stopped by loud shouts, two policemen lay my attacker down and he was very excited, they have clear orders that a hair should be crumbed. They went away with him, I remained.

But they did not close the door. Strange. They are not trained for this, I'm beginning to look around, this is unlike anything I've ever seen of cells. Walls of gray concrete. No windows, a single bulb under a grille in the ceiling and the strangest of all: a huge wooden bench filling almost the entire cell. It is one and a half meters high, slightly sloping down in front towards the floor so limited that you could barely walk back and forth and I speculate on why? when they came back for me.

Along the prison corridor to a small table, an officer behind a lamp with a protocol in front of him. Then the officers derive me of the usual and useful stuff – everything you need waiting in a cell: A watch to keep up with infinity, matches to light cigarettes, and a wallet with plenty of reading stuff in it, belts and shoelaces to make a rope with and then the shoes. To walk away in.

Then they close the door.

The inside of the door is massive. No bars, no windows. But instead of a keyhole there is a small space in the woodwork, enough to obtain small glances of life outside the cell, and it would save me through the night. For now I crawl up on the bench, fold my jacket to a pillow, tuck it under my head and fall asleep. And notice nothing when someone shook my shoulder. But finally I woke up and had everything ready, the officers talked a lot but gave me only my lace–less shoes and nothing more. We're going to another place in the same building.

A few floors up and into an office. Behind a moderately intimidating desk sat a middle–aged civilian, this is routine for him and they need all the *personalia* and all that in order to pass a preliminary charge so that nobody can come and claim that this is a rogue and lawless state run by buccaneers. At the end of the table a young and beautiful woman was sitting, I was lead to a chair.

A young and beautiful woman! Then there were even such women in this world as well, such a woman amongst the KGB and the police. She is a redhead, a few years older than me and could have been from Fredrikstad. The man nods his head slightly, she presents herself, in Swedish:

– My name is Katarina and I am an interpreter (*perivodsjik, basjalst!*), this is the prison leader with a long and terrible name, and he will make the necessary record of your belongings, take down your personal details and ask a few questions. He emphasizes that this is not an interrogation. It will take place tomorrow, as you will be moved. And he is very sorry that they were unable to obtain a Norwegian interpreter so quickly, and he wants to know if it is ok with a Swedish interpreter? Because if so, they can use me in future sessions as well?

This beautiful creature, and I think that yes, by all means and answer:

– Yes, by all means.

The following were boring and routine and with an utmost accuracy, Katarina was smiling nicely and looking me straight in the eyes and me o my! They had my trunk and all its contents, all noted and nodded and confirmed and time goes by, I protested now and then and time goes by, I thought of the long and dark night.

The officer in charge showed me a flyer and asked if I confess it, which I acknowledge.

– We know you had an accomplice. His name is Alex Langberg, where is he?

– He had problems with his ulcer and wanted to return to Denmark. So he took the plane home.

He thereby told me that they know that I know and that they do not bother to play any game. There is a limit to everything. Suddenly it strikes me that Axel really *was* sick and how would I have liked to be hospitalized in a foreign country? A prison hospital even? I winced and blushed heavily.

I confirmed that I am aware of the contents of the flyer, that I voluntarily and knowingly had scattered them in Leningrad, I thus had initiated an illegal demonstration and I was prepared for this and had both the UN Human Rights and the Soviet constitution ready to my support but he interrupted:

– Just answer yes or no.

At this point someone brought in some food. A plate of sandwiches and a pot of coffee. The prison leader invited me to eat, but I said well no thanks, just coffee.

– No thanks! Is the Russian food not good enough for you?

– I'm on a hunger strike.

He suddenly looked very funny. Quiet and strange in his face, and I realized that this was obviously something new, definitely this was mot used by protesters before. No wonder I was intended for the trial the guys back home so dearly wanted. But then his face fell back to normal, and he had decided: this is so not my problem!

– But why?

– To support our claim for the full release of Grikorenko and Galanskov.

– Well, then we can proceed.

He rose calmly and composed, and up came the same declaration from earlier today, now in an English version, and pretty much the same procedure. But he knew perfectly well how very useless it was, he had done his job and it was all over. He actually greeted me and shook my hand, I got to hold Katarina's small and warm hand for a brief moment, then I was led out.

On the way down we visited a photographer and my fingerprints were taken. So back to my cell and the long and winding night.

I was no longer tired after a nap and some coffee, it was possible to sit on the bench in the far corner and thus have the support of both the walls and even some space left for the head. I had a lot of things to sort out, time passed by, but slowly it began to settle. Then came the real night, they turned off the silly lamp! The sudden darkness left me almost unconscious, I was in the middle of nowhere and was I dead or alive? I had never offered death one thought in my life, and could this be the right place and the right time? I could not just sit all night long in jail and think non–existing words like the hero of Knut Hamsun's *Hunger* made up as time goes by... what a strange association ...

Then I caught a glimpse of this little split strip of light through the door, this little string of reminder about the world outside. I moved towards the light so it hit my cheek, everything was comfortable and I was myself and me and my sat in a cell. Again.

But soon a new day is dawning after one day in prison in the Soviet Union as well as in the United States. Where I have also been arrested. As a young sailor I was once arrested in Portland, Oregon. I was a guide for two of my thirsty shipmates – they did not speak a word of English. But already I was an unbearable intellectual, I was mugged for my book reading when at sea, but in ports my knowledge came in handy. I was not quite as plastered as my friends, but when they drank directly out of the bottle, an officer blew his whistle and *smack*! in the locker. I managed to get my one phone–call, got hold of the ship's agent in town, he provided a counselor, we pleaded guilty and was sentenced to sixty days suspended for public drinking. Way to go! But not a word of my career as a Norwegian drunk'n & jailbird in Norway. But later ... For here comes the food. I'm a bit puzzled. I'm in jail. There is no breakfast served here, this is no bed & breakfast because the clients usually manage to deal with the liquids, and food is of little interest, so one do not get breakfast here.

I did.

Not much, just some bread, some butter, and cheese, and a small sausage, perhaps? And coffee. The rumor has already spread, phones have been ringing and now they have called for catering and the door is open oddly enough but the coffee is really good.

And I'm hungry. But no more than usual. Play it again, Sam, this will be some easy pieces. But since I am off cakes, I park the food, confirm that I have neither smoke or matches, but I know that already. And after a little unbearable eternity it strikes me that my employees rather should have been looking for nonsmokers; if this situation should continue I'm willing to sign anything, especially on a cigarette paper for example. But here and now I just shake my head and shrug my shoulders a little. Short loss, long suffering.

The hours were passing. But what the hell! I forgot to present my main claim! How did the *listo* go, the flyer, the text that George had taught me on the sofa back in Oslo! So I started off:

– *Svaboda Grigarjenka, svaboda Galnskov, sva ...*

Fairly quickly a couple of guys started pounding at my door, they have heard what I have been brought in for, because otherwise they would have unlocked the door. I realize that the choice of time and place were somewhat questionable, and that the protest was over. It was too late for speeches. Time is up, now I'm down.

I am down and inside, but soon I'm out. For around two'ish I was picked up and finally I got my shoelaces back. Two civilians this time, I was upgraded to category significant, that is worrisome. Armored conveyance with racks and officers, I fetched a cig and asked nicely with my eyes, one polite nod, I smoked a couple of fags simultaneously and quick as a cigarette, the trip was over.

Into a courthouse. This was certainly a preliminary hearing more than an interrogation, they would surely follow the book and really there was not much to ask me about. I thought. This *was* no preliminary hearing, this *was* an interrogation. A somewhat strange interrogation: Discreetly located was a three–flight rack with suspiciously delicious sandwiches, very fresh they were, Danish pastry, fresh they were and the smell ... I got stuck in the aroma of coffee.

– Gunnar Gjengset, a student born in 1946 in Trondheim, Norway – all personal data that previously was duly noted – you have even signed and acknowledged the preliminary interrogation yesterday.

He handed me a sheet in English, it was true that I signed it, completed as it was on beforehand. But I checked it to see if they had engaged in some magic. I confirmed that it was okay, he raised himself a little in the chair, we could get started. And we, then, was I, my inquisitor, two men in plainclothes, probably the same two who had brought me here, and no interpreter. I hesitated a bit. No interpreter? No interpreter, because he had addressed me in English.

I was chilled, tried to turn my head slightly to see if there was someone in the background, making notes, at least. He knew perfectly well what I thought and explained mildly:

– This is not a court, so we do not need to take down the minutes. This is just a conversation around some details that are a little shady to us, but completely off the record. And do help yourself to some food, here is some mineral water, tea and coffee. And sandwiches.

Pure torture, in other words. Sandwich–torture. I was sandwiched between hunger and well dressed ... sandwiches. Or so I thought in order to tighten up myself a bit, of course, my spirits were really pretty low. Still, I assumed that I had nothing to fear physically, they could simply not risk the strain. To return a badly mutilated westerner was particularly not smart, even accounts of physical pressure was unwanted. My hand was not quite steady when I poured my coffee:

– I would like to ask for a lawyer if I am accused. If I am not indicted, I would like to immediately get in touch with my embassy.

– You have not yet been indicted. You need no lawyer. You will of course get in touch with your embassy as soon as your status is clarified ....

What the hell did he mean ... my status? I was accused, or was I not? What other kind of mess could they make?

– You have previously rejected an offer of automatic deportation for your improper misconduct. So probably it is of no use to repeat the offer, but I will do it anyway: To avoid measures of another nature, I would recommend you to consent to the signing of the document you already know, and subsequently you then are a free man. Well, almost, we have to follow you to the door.

– I repeat that I do not want to utter anything before I get in touch with the embassy.

He replied:

– The faster you cooperate, the faster we call the embassy.

I stirred the coffee and thought some more about the sugar that was luring in front of me. I could also take a little milk, perhaps? Then I imagined the reaction – one civilian galloping to the telegraph and all over Europe, the message was: "The Norwegian activist has aborted his hunger strike! In confidential talks with officials from the Ministry of the Interior he drank some coffee with cream and sugar." Aiaiai how complicated this would become. Had we discussed this, or? Tea, for example, was it allowed with sugar in the tea? I hate tea without sugar and knows very well that we have discussed it: no sugar, no lump of sugar. No nothing. *Njeta.*

– I cannot answer anything else but my name and number, and I can also confirm what I already have confirmed about the facts. Comments beyond this, I will not give without a lawyer or someone form my embassy present.

At least I could annoy them as long as possible, put on the superior image that we boys from the bourgeoisie are so good at and bloody hell how bad that coffee was. And yet I had not understood what they were looking for.

– We know that you represent a group called SMOG, and he pronounced the Russian words of the acronym.

– But this is obviously just an excuse. If this group should be as concerned with the suppression of human rights, how is it then that you only demonstrate in the USSR? Such repression do not take place here with us, of course, but in many other countries.

– Our organization's main mission is the oppression in the Soviet Union. Other groups are working with other countries, Chile, for example; and then we use the benefits of the Amnesty International as our umbrella organization. We concentrate on the Soviet Union.

– Here we *support* the human rights. No one is imprisoned for his convictions. It is enshrined in the Constitution. We have also ratified the UN Human Rights.

Signed, I thought. Not ratified, signed. It's absolutely absurd that he uses my arguments, I had not been prepared for this discussion at this time, and decided to stick to the formalities. When I later told George about this situation, there suddenly was a demonstration against the junta in Greece, signed SMOG. Too funny, too late.

– I will only refer to what I …

– We know that SMOG is just a cover organization for the NTS. We want to know what contacts you have, where you've been, who you've met, future plans and so on.

A totally unexpected development. "They will not ask for NTS," Mike had said, "because then they must admit that the NTS exists, and that means they are desperate," and it meant a whole lot of trouble for me. But what had he really admitted? That I would not know anything more about them than I could give away, than what was freely accessible. "But if they play the NTS card, you will be the last demonstrator. And if you keep your mouth shut, you are guaranteed a trial, I think. And thereby confirm that this will be the last demonstration, NTS or not." Trial it will be – something wicked this way comes …. Huhei.

– I repeat that I …

We kept it going on like this for hours. We from Trondheim can be incredibly stubborn.

– We do know that you have been in the United States several times. Can you tell me what you were doing there?

– I was there as a sailor. For the most part in New York.

– Tell us about your trip to the West Coast.

Now I really started to sweat. They were damned well oriented. KGB were no fools, as Mike had said. And this was even at a higher level, this was the Ministry. But how much did they really know?

– I wanted to visit a friend of mine, Mike, he had been a year in my class as an exchange student, who lives in. ..

– ... San José, close to Silicon Valley. Was he the one who asked you to visit him?

An unexpected twist. They believe we are the ones who love America. I realized that this was only gestures, they were trying to equip young Mike as covert CIA and me as a ditto useful idiot. What they did not know was that Mike was a Navajo Indian and a crypto–Communist as they called it in America in the 1950s, but they knew that I was not a useful idiot. Or maybe I was? But if so to whom? Maybe it was the dull hunger that made me a little fuzzy in eye and mind, but I pushed it aside for future deliberations. NTS ran a legitimate resistance struggle by whatever means they found appropriate, and SMOG was expedient. I was representing SMOG and knew no other, they would only try to deceive me into a network that I was not able to entacle. I took a calculated risk:

– I regret that I allowed myself to derail for a moment, I repeat that I would like to be in contact with my embassy, or that I am read my rights so that I can get in touch with a lawyer.

They had apparently given up.

– We understand that you have begun a hunger strike. What is the purpose?

– The objective is the immediate release of Galanskov and Grigorenko, and my hunger strike will be maintained as long as I am on Soviet soil.

They conferred for a moment, they had apparently anticipated this. But they did have to give it a shot. So to speak.

– To be able to guarantee the best possible care for your health, you will be detained in a hospital for the time you are going to stay here, or until we have reached upon a decision about the sanctions that are appropriate for your ... errors. You will be taken directly to Kuybysjev hospital.

13

WELCOME TO THE CRIMINAL ASYLUM

Kuybysjev hospital.

Not quite so: The Kuybysjev *criminal* asylum. As the director kindly explained to me later, someone who had demonstrated against the political system in the Soviet Union would necessarily be deranged.

I have no idea where it is situated or what it looks like, I arrived in an armored car. The access was somewhat more gently than a prison would offer, but the intake procedures were the same. Again my shoelaces and everything else was removed. I was gradually stripped down on my way downwards through the floors, I was more than grounded, actually undergrounded, where they held the most craziest. At the last of bolted gates, my underpants disappeared. My last shred of dignity was taken away from me.

All I got was a pajamas and a bathrobe.

A stench of sheer despair hit me. No ordinary smell of hospital, here they did not even bother to medicate their guests. Not exactly guests, no one were let out alive from here. Last stop and thank you and goodbye. Two men in white robes escorted me down the hall. Green walls, jail-green walls that would stick to your last remnants of wits and senses. On my right hand were four doors: three for toilets, one for shower. A shower for how many?

Too many. They are locked up on the left side of the corridor. Out from behind this series of doors, oozed all the sounds that you would recognize from mental hospitals in the 50s. Loud screams, slow monotone chanting, short howls and a woman who believes she is a seagull. The first time heard it, I jumped and looked for the damn gulls, but after a time that sounds gave me the kind of maritime peace. As a foghorn always make me fall asleep.

Bottom right was my room. They gave me a single room. They intend to treat me well, but they scare me a bit. And here I am sitting utterly alone beyond time and space in a reality that none of us had ever suggested before I embarked on this journey.

Then nothing happens. Then begins the Nothingness–week.

What happens is that I have to pee. All the time I have to pee. I have not eaten solid food for more than fourteen days, at least not since ... and already I began to lose the grip of time. But first – pee! I'm pounding on the door, for there is no bucket here. There's nothing in here, and I have to drink water from the tap while I'm on the toilet. And time goes by – water out, water in. Water out, water in. All who are starting on a diet know about this, but they at least have a toilet handy. Not me, and immediately I learned the importance of *"toilet, basjalst!"* While I was thinking of the time passed, I concluded that I demonstrated on Thursday, since then it has passed ... one night. Oh my God, no more?

This is the first day of your new life.

It's an expression I surely never use. My life was not meant to be like this – in and out of the bathroom in between thoughts about the future. Nevertheless, I had full confidence in the situation. This was true and real isolation, in solitary confinement. But a proper insulation means the absence of all sound, light, and thus time. It is the ultimate infinity, and those who speak of eternity should be locked up immediately. Maybe they will then understand the enormity of the idea, for knowing that something will never end, is unbearable. Being alone in infinity must be even worse than the unbearable, and isolation is humanity's worst torture. It never ends. When they remove time, the torture never ends. After all, physical pain is limited by time.

Knock, knock! Someone's paying a visit! No, nobody knocks. They do not knock, they rattle with their key ring, and they bring food. They have received a ban on fraternizing with the culprit, but I'll bet that they knew everything about me. Walls are no obstacles to the rumors in Russia. So they bring on the food and can't help it.

And the smells. Cabbage and gasoline. Cabbage from the bowl, gasoline from the window. A few pieces of black bread and water. A spoon. The water in a pot of steel. It is not picked up before it is empty, therefore: I learn to ration. Strange, but they did not tempt me more than this. But they expect that I am sufficiently well–fed, so they do not need to waste expensive cuts of meat that still did not get eaten. I have also heard that fasting was good, it cleans up and is leading all the slag out of the body and here I go again, to the door, *toilet basjalst* and shock–shock to the loo. For I have also been set up with a kind of slippers, and then back again. I waste as much time as possible, time passes, time goes by, moreover it is good to stretch one's legs. Amazing how quickly one learns to adapt, I figured – a bit scared.

No one comes to visit. Of course, I have been making fuss about lawyers and embassies and police and fire departments, but nothing seemed to help. Maybe that explained why they did not bring in catering here; lack of food that will not break me, but the lack of contact will. In this case, quite smart. In my situation, I am isolated times two: solitary confinement, and without sufficient language.

But otherwise, I have a plentiful of activities. Just take a look at the area! The floor must be measured accurately: Six and a half feet one way, four feet the other. Or vice versa. Or was it six? Trying again: Six and a half feet. Then there were the walls. Make a note: Not to be walked. These feet were made for walking ... And time is falling out completely from time to time. There is silence inside of me, my head is empty, I recap scenes from another time and where was I wandering? Actually, a little on the outside of the so–called reality. And I decided to write the novel *Going for a drive with my father.*

But then I would need some paper. That word, I have recently learned. I'm pounding on the door and shouting *"bumagi basjalst!",* and eventually they come dragging along, meaning only one of them is coming, they've decided that I'm not crazy, but on the contrary, the political activist they have heard rumors about and how do they handle that? I imagine that most of those imprisoned over here are not exactly sitting on the lap of Uncle Brezhnev. The ward gave me a little piece of toilet paper. I explained that it was not that kind of paper I had in mind, I needed paper for writing and made a pantomime out of it. But he just shook his head.

They brought a toothbrush and I realized that it was evening. It is not my toothbrush, it is not my toilet equipment: they offer me a towel in a canvaslike fabric and a piece of vet–soap.

It's time for my first visit to the bathroom. Untreated concrete floors and ditto walls, no window, ten to twelve double showers in a number of wooden boards in the middle of the floor. Along one wall two basins as well as mirrors. But the water was hot. I make myself ready and make the evening's last trip to the john. When I had finished and was about to walk back to my cell, I noticed that all the cells in the corridors are open. No wonders, the inmates here are not going anywhere and it's just to facilitate the job of the wardens they are locked up during the day. The shower is occupied and more than so. There are inmates of two cells at once in there. Both sexes, all naked. They might be heavily medicated by their looks – heavy lethargy, strong sedatives. They are not interested in each other, they are interested in the water, they are pressed together in the cells days or weeks on end, and I expect there is one week between each shower.

I count sixteen.

Two cells are empty, eight men in one and eight women in the other. I am looking into the empty cells. They are as big as mine. The interior is a miracle, there are actually four berths in the height of each wall. Same green walls, the lights in the ceiling, the same nothing as my cell. But *eight*! Now I must also begin to count the square centimeters per prisoner to fathom the luxury I have all to myself. Even when isolated there are some positive aspects to be found. Incredible!

Back in my cell a long time passed, whatever that is, because I had lost the track of it ... until I remembered my intention to write a book. Just call room service, I was pounding at the door and *bumagi* I claimed and made writing movements, he shook his head decisively and slammed the door shut. Enough for today, he thought. Enough for today, I thought.

14

HUNGER STRIKE – A MATTER OF WILL

And there was evening, and there was morning–the third day. And there is nothing divine about it.

My third day in prison, four days in custody. Next day nothing happened. And it was surely intended. They achieved two things: first, to determine if I was really hungry, and second, simply to torture me a bit. See how I tackled *lone–li–ness*. No one to talk to, no intelligible ones to talk to. It was the same monosyllables, the same rush of lawyers, the same *ni panjimai*, I do not understand, water in, water out, food in, food out while I kept the brown heated stuff they served. I was never able to determine whether it was tea or coffee. Same shit, it made me feel good. Not cappuccino in a moment like this, give him the swamp–ish–ness!

And then my thoughts went around in circles that got narrower and narrower and I began to wonder how long I could survive without a partner, before going off the rocker. Already, I started talking to myself, just to hear a speech delivered with some length and never shall I giggle of people walking on the street and conversation themselves. And this was more than twenty years ahead of the cell phones. And suddenly I understand the true meaning of *cell phone* – not *cellular*, but *the user is confined to his own cell*. As I was.

On the third day of hunger strike, hunger was not troublesome any more. Sometimes flairs of hunger, but not annoying. If you have sufficient water everything would be okay, but I had not, wherefore I had to be inventive to interrupt the gnawing. But again, piece of .... A milder disorder that would meet its end. But how close was the end? That was, also in the end, my own decision, I was told. As soon as the press had presented the hunger strike, it would be on until the start of the trial. For they could not start the trial with me dieting. They recommended striking for some seven to ten days, depending on what I could stomach. We had a good laugh from that expression.

Today I am going to learn more about this. The trustee of the prison entered. It turned out that my guards were also prisoners, but as they had behaved well, they had been granted this privilege of assisting the jailers here. The prison's trustee is thus also these boys' trustee, and he had this invaluable advantage of knowing some German. A little. He brought along my clothes, trousers and jacket and shoes – with laces! Plus an electric shaver and a small hand mirror.

– The director wants to talk to you. Do not eat? Dangerous, very dangerous. Not good food but eat, or ...

He pretended that he staked out a drain, with both hands. I pretended I did not understand, he didn't literally mean plumbing. I had perhaps imagined that they could break a hunger strike by artificial feeding, but had only vague opinions about what that really would be like. Something with white sheets and mild nurses and such. I threw it aside, and I went along to the director, this seemed like a good day for talking to directors. He whispered to me:

– *Wir sind ja imponiert. Mutig!* Listov, *ajajaj!*

(We are impressed. Courage! Leaflets ... !)

In fact this was the first time I heard this word *listov*, the closest to *flyer* in Russian, but it was the main topic during the trial, in some ways. I thought that this could be a useful contact. The trustee was right in his fifties, was in his own clothes and always had a soft shell jacket and fur cap on, a scabby reef by the look of it. But always pleasant and obliging the times I met him.

The director was called Smirnoff. He was bald and slightly corpulent, in a rather modest office. Nothing much to speak for, ending up as director of a madhouse. He was sharp but generous, as his name. Smirnoff, by the way, are the Smiths of Russia. He was presented by the interpreter, Olga. That was certainly not her name, but I remember her as Olga. She looked like that. The only thing she had in common with Katarina was a touch of reddish hair, she was certainly not attractive and looked like the Komsomol forever. But she interpreted in a proper Norwegian, not more than proper:

– My name is Olga and I will be your interpreter from now on. This is the director Oleg Petrovich Smirnoff, he has some questions for you.

Henceforth followed some polite chat, he could not very well ask if there was anything I wanted – but then he quickly came to the point:

– As far as we understand you are staging a hunger strike. How long do you intend to continue?

– Until my demands are followed up, the release of …

– Well, we know all that, he broke off.

But I had been so looking forward to hearing Komsomolskaja Olga perform my appeal in a precise translation. He was also bringing on the table this document for me to sign but only halfheartedly, he well understood that one do not halt free running horses with paper.

– As you know, this strike is completely useless. There is no one outside of Leningrad who has heard about you, and for that matter, you can starve as long as you have the strength. But since we are human, we're going to break the hunger strike to prevent serious complications.

I wondered for whom? But this was serious business, and I almost forgot my automatic reply:

– I note that I am, in my opinion, illegally held in custody without trial, and I do ask for contact with my embassy immediately. If I'm accused of something, I am also asking for a lawyer, these being rights that you, as a lawyer, knows very well that I am entitled to.

Sheer luck. He *was* a lawyer. Actually, I asked to learn whether he was a psychiatrist, but they tend to always hide behind white coats. Which Smirnof did not. And then I would be very afraid. Psychiatrists are dangerous because they think they know what they are doing. But the director wore his dull grayish lawyerlike suit, and it matched. Because now we shared similar codes; my car owning father was a lawyer and I almost became one myself. That's why I took a degree in political science.

– It's true that I am a lawyer, and I can state that we are on safe ground when we keep you here. Currently you are here in thisinstitution for us to make a report, we have to determine your diagnosis and then possibly decide whether you will be accused. And in that moment you will of course get in touch with your embassy, which will appoint an appropriate attorney on a free basis.

They are in a hurry! It is seething and boiling in Fleet Street and Stop the Press –cafes, Amnesty's beating their drums and just outside here a new group is posing every day just to get towed away but at least they are in a hurry and I am not able to decide if it is good or bad. It does not matter here and now. Smirnoff can swear as much as he will that no one cares about me in the west; if that really was the case, nobody would have cared about me here in the east but now everybody cares! I swallow a lump in the throat and am enjoying the second: Never again will I find myself as cared about as now.

– For your own sake, I will advise you to end the hunger strike as soon as possible. First and foremost for your own sake, but our patience has its limits. I emphasize that this is a recommendation and not a threat. But if you on a free basis do not resume normal intake of food, the prison's medical management will make the right decision about what actions must be implemented.

– I affirm my decision to strike by starving and I am ready to take the consequences this may have for my person.

– Then I consider this conversation is over. The trustee will follow you back to your cell, and we will resume this conversation at a more convenient time.

Laconic. But so far I have met very few rock faces beneath the balustrades of the Kremlin. The people live their own lives, they breed and love and drink and enjoy themselves, struggling with their jobs as we do, fighting with the spouse and children and cursing the tiny apartment and the meat they never obtain and standing in line after line. But living their lives, reading the Pravda and constructing their own myths, politely listening to the radio and immediately creating their own – weather forecasts they get on TV, the truth they conceive on *Radio Yerevan*. A nation of ironics! I might as well defect on the spot.

This is a moment for a smoke! My trustee has been sitting in there and overheard everything, he is deeply worried.

– *Nicht gut*, he mumbles. *Sehr schlecht*.

He is in a bad mood, but now I'm ready, I'm not going to rot hidden and forgotten in Lubjanka, the dreaded prison for the damned of the earth. It worries me less what will happen, but I know by the trustee's conduct that it will be something very specific, and not necessarily pleasant. This is the right moment:

– *Mag ich bitte ein Cigarett haben? Bitte?* (May I have a cigarette? Please?)

My German is about leveling the trustee's, but the content is the message. He just keeps on growling, followed me back to my cell, and left me mildly intoxicated. I think about life in the sea. This conversation has made me very restless, I've learned that everything has its end but here time is endless. I'm struggling a bit with the grille in front of the window, feeling the air being crisp today and suddenly the door opened, and for the first time I hear:

– *Kurrits, basjalst!*

Afterwards I lie on the bunk, sensing peace and medium risk. This daily walk with my sentry the Hamsun–lover, apparently is mandatory, there's something about the rules and regulations and such, but only today we are polluting the air. I'm still right in the middle of the trap, but there has been a little hustle and bustle and expectations around it. My head is just as easy and transparent as several days of fasting will lead to, and last night I slept for hours. I'm starting to get used to the sounds, it's quieter at night and the inmates apparently are served extra pills in the evening, I believe. If they do not downright turn off the lights in the other cells. Not in mine: The light is always on. One glaring bulb of at least 250 watts, impossible to protect against. I can't be bothered to check.

However, someone is screaming once in a while. First we have the gull, but then I just rolled on into sleep. Nothing makes me sleep better than the sound of a foghorn. Sea vicinity, childhood safety. Then we have Diva. At first I called her actress, but it was too cumbersome to check in my busy life. I knew nothing of her, but it can't be a coincidence that her screams were so sonorous and stylish and do I recognize an aria in there? Maybe a Stalin relic, Sholokov's secret lover or simply a whore mama that went bankrupt. Here in the quiet of the night, the possibilities were many.

Things were getting worse when Frankenstein began to pound his head into the walls and floors. He keeps on until a couple of guards pick him up, he was huge and his face full of stitches that made him look like he has had his head sewn on. Hence the name. He is led away, and then the silence is deafening. I'm guessing that he is led to the uttermost extreme place where he is strapped with the misty remnants of his mind.

All this is possible and all this happened. But there is a rhythm in everything, and sleep is always seeking towards that rhythm. And with my head under my blanket, I discovered that they are not as aggressively on the look through the peeping hole at night, just as a routine every now and then, sometimes I hear that *swish!* one eye looking through the keyhole. And they leave me and my head in peace under the blanket. One can take away everything, but this is only the first circle.

I get more visits. It is actually Olga. She brought a nurse, who said she was only collecting a blood sample from me. It was completely harmless, and just something they forgot during my medical examination. But the interpreter came down here on her own, she must be highly trusted. If this is the idea of a honey trap, they should have found a better queen.

Now here was this lovable little creature that would draw some blood. It is a straightforward and clean case. But she had no needles and rubber cord and pump and whatever is needed. However, a normal tin bowl. And somewhere in there a bunch of sterilized pen nibs. Aha – not blood but Pirque. A small interpreter's error.

No interpreter's errors. She sat down beside me quite friendly, but determined when she took one of my arms between her two. Then she took hold of the wrist of my right arm, tightened her grip on my thumb and stuck a pen split into it. Hell, painful! She squeezed out a drop of blood and this antiquated method, they just revived in order to tease me. Not that simple. After she had finished with the index finger and prepared for the long one, I realized that this was merely a warning. They pinned up a drawing of real torture for me with my own blood, they drained the blood from every finger and in complete amazement I automatically reached out my left arm. But by then she was done, many thanks, and full of cotton and strange thoughts I stumbled back into my cell.

15

EMIL UND DIE DETEKTIVE

Day four in here, day five dieting.

Tuesday, January 27, 1970. The Soviet national anthem reverberates through the corridors, the rattling of keys and tin bowls and the time is again set in motion and I look forward to the breakfast I soon will not eat and wonder what eating habits did my corridor mates have? Coziness was invading me, blocking out the alarming fact that I was detained in a loony bin, surrounded not only by insane, but by insane *criminals* – I desperately needed a reality check:

What's the worst that can happen?

They may torment you physically, but they will not. They can make you stay here for life, but they will not. They can send you to Siberia, and perhaps they will. But that would be interesting, I like to travel. The worst that can happen is therefore endurable. And slowly I opened my eyes and began looking forward to timely businesses and the possibility of regular walks with cigarettes. Also there were far worse places in which to put people in this country. For example *Lubjanka*, it is the place you put people that you really would rather forget. Then hey are forgotten. I was treated with the utmost delicacy, I had a whole regimen in my pocket that only was interested in the fact that was am alive and well. For they were going to have to treat me well, otherwise I would not be sitting here warm and dry and protected.

I did not shiver with cold. I did not perish from hunger or pain. Outside the world was spinning and could tell me how it did look today by looking through my window, there were bars in front of them and I was sitting in the basement so only partially I got to see day and night and the glare of the sun, I could hear the rain drops and the whining from the trams and cars and gasoline. I see and hear, I remember and will not be forgotten. I am a tiny cog in a game that is too large. Others can tell tales of prison hell. I can not. Because of the care I am enjoying, I can not. I was given a lifeline to hold on to, I was staying afloat, I did not sink to the bottom.

But today things were happening. Two big matters. I had noticed that the atmosphere had become more relaxed, the orderlies are openly friendly with me. Yesterday I just caught a glimpse of the outside world when the *Leningradskaya Pravda* suddenly appeared. It was Pjotr who came with it. Pyotr, *Peter the Straight*. The director had asserted that nobody outside Leningrad knew about my demonstration, but surely they knew about it here. So well known was the action that the party tried neutralizing it with an article for anyone to read. I suspected I had the trustee to thank for this sudden information, but they had to be careful: the newspaper was quickly snatched away. But I will never forget it. The entire paper just one *flake*, as the Norwegian expression goes: approximately one square meter of paper folded into four times two: Making a total of 8 pages. And the main headline on page three:
ФИАСКО ГУННЕРА ГЪЕНГСЕТА (The Fiasko of Gunnar Gjengset). This was on February 11, 1970.

After breakfast Pyotr came back in again. He brought with him two books, two copies of the same book. He gave me one and said something about *panjimaj* and *gavarui* that had to do with *understand* and *talk*, clearly he meant something specific with this. And he did, they are textbooks in German, books for kids with German text on the left side and Russian on the right. I understood immediately how he was thinking: With some help and guidance we will together create an increased understanding, we should be able to climb laboriously from one word to another, from one world to another, and thus simply understand. Peace and friendship in practice: **М И Р   И   Д Р У Щ Ъ В А** or *Mir drusjba.* And the book?

Emil und die Detektive.

Deeply touched I sat on the bed and could not see clearly for several minutes. Erich Kästner is my favorite writer of all time – I scrolled back and forth in the book and this chapter fell immediately open to "*Emil steigt an der falschen Station aus*" (Emil entered at the wrong station), I thought about my own diversionary maneuvers outside Moscow and it was almost eerie how all this were reflections of my own situation and only the chapter list gave an overall presentation of my travels and adventures in Wonderland and I was especially looking forward to the chapter "*Die Reise nach Berlin kann los gehen*" (Starting on a trip to Berlin), and a nightly extradition between east and west on a bridge over the Elbe and finally the end chapter, "*Lässt sich daraus was lernen?*" (What can be learned from this?).

But we should be learning languages. Not losing ourselves in scary stories about mixing up trains and spies sneaking into hotels in various cities, "*Ein Spion schleicht ins Hotel*", (A spy turns up in the hotel); here we were down to basics, each specific word. Such as *bread*. Right in front of me, from my uneaten breakfast. I looked it up the dictionary and found **Ж Л Е В** , *chleb.* This Cyrillic *x* is the missing Russian *h,* and is an impossible uvula–vault and sounds like *ch.* So *chleb.*

Next year I would find the same word in Finnmark. I ran away from the world and found the Sami people, they ate bread and called it *Leibe.* The world is full of bread and language. For in an ancient version of Norwegian, bread is called *leiv.* Small world, narrow cell.

We are making rapid progress. We were getting much aid from the dictionaries, and we hurried directly to two–word sentences in normal language development. He said that they know everything about my action; most of the guards are regular prison officers, some of the medical staff would occasionally come down here to this Court of Death as they call it. Sounded a bit eternal, but as I understand even Pyotr would not get out for a while, unlike the regular employees going to and fro, bringing in fresh news every day. Moreover, he was not sentenced incommunicado.

Incommunicado!

What a wonderful word. Here I was, suffering from incommunicado. As if I was in Mexico. Confined as the worst crook amongst murderers of the first degree, I was placed in solitary confinement with restrictions on visits and correspondence times two: Those who may not visit me, I cannot understand, and what I do not get to read, I cannot understand. But Pyotr is a prisoner himself and offers me no letters or visits, he does what he is sentenced to, he is doing his damned duty.

Convicted of stealing a radio. He worked in a radio factory and maybe it was a girlfriend he wanted to impress, it was something about *ljub* deep in the phrase somewhere and it has something to do with *love* , and here I have to fill in the story on my own. But he stole the radio, and it ended in disaster: He was sentenced to five years in prison. Five years: *pjat goda*. My goodness!

It could not be. I mean – my own penalty would be from three to five years, depending on what they chose to charge me with; and my crime was, after all, of the more serious variety. The answer could only be that they operated with two sets of laws: The one that was written down, and the other was the one that they practiced. Not easy to live in such a system, here it was almost impossible to face the existence at ... face value. I tried to articulate something about how long time to serve he had left, and finally we were down to two. Two years left. Maybe we would be released at the same time. But this was a too complicated sentence to put together, rather something for my exams of this intensive course.

School hours were extremely irregular. He had to sneak in and steal a few minutes here and there from the employer, I had my hands full with Emil and my head full of language and life was just sing and dance. Out of this man's incredible ingenuity sheer conversations might develop, he could reveal secrets of the unfortunate surrounding for me, I could convey lies about Norway, just about everything that existed on the other side of the border are legends and fairy tales to the average Russians and therefore lies. But lies are always promising.

In a situation such as this, I could spend much of my life: Learning and teaching, reading and creating stories. In this way this mythical landscape was woven together into a large and complex tapestry that ultimately would be understandable. Then we could soar above it all, like on a flying carpet, with overview and insight in all things hidden and covert, soaring soaring Pyotr and Gunnar and the walls around us were only our friendly protection against the cold.

It's easy to daydream in prisons. One has not much else: dreams and procedures. I only had dreams, now I got routines and the day is all about the highlight of the walk in the courtyard and time goes by, at six o'clock in the morning time was ignited by the Soviet national anthem over the intercom and the time goes by, it did not exactly run along but was strolling along at a fair pace and in the middle of all this movement a nice stack of paper was also coming my way, the trustee had heard my pleadings and single–handedly handed me a stack of paper, three sheets of paper and a pencil. But the confession I announced I intended to write was so difficult to write, I had to practice a bit first, and none of them knew anything of what I was writing, so I had to apply the world's smallest font and only I was able to read those signs that were less than memories of a small crow's toes.

But on the seventh day of they struck. Eight days without food and seven days with increasing well–being here in my room – I have forgotten the world that existed outside of the binders of *Emil und die Detektive* as I approached the next chapter, "*Die Detective versammeln sich.*" (The detectives came together). But by now the police outside the binders were gathering. Thursday, January 29, they gathered in the room for medical treatment in the corridor. Treatment was on its way.

They waited for me.

ЛЕНИНГРАДСКАЯ ПРАВДА

11 февраля 1970 г.

ФИАСКО ГУННЕРА ГЬЕНГСЕТА

ИЗ ЗАЛА СУДА

Редактор В. С. КУРТЫНИН

"Fiasko Gunnera Gjengseta", from the
Leningradskaja Pravda, 11th of February 1970.

16

WILL AND ITS BOUNDARIES

The game is over.

I am lead into a room, a mixture of a room for visits and treatment. A single sofa, and the place where the warders are reading their newspapers and drinking mugs with memories of coffee. Full ashtrays. Behind a half–wall first aid equipment is to be found, some glass cabinets and an examination bench, with belts.

The warden is there, as well as the trustee and the interpreter. Finally, a charge will be presented, I hope; finally some action, changes in routine is only a delight. The warden:

– We understand that you still maintain the hunger strike, and therefore we have only two matters to ask you about. I have been told by the trustee here that you have paper to write a confession on, or a statement. Have you written a confession, or are you now willing to sign the statement you know about?

– I have nothing new to add, and any confession must of course be presented to my counselor first. Appoint a lawyer for me, then we'll see.

– Well. It is obviously not appropriate for the authorities even to consider the character of your requirements, both mentioned in your ... petition are legally detained and, consequently, no arrangements will be made. Will you still continue your hunger strike?

– The warden knows the answer to that question.

The interpreter translated. The Director appealed directly to the trustee and swore him in as a witness to what was being said:

– Is it correct that you intend to continue the hunger strike?

– Yes.

– Please, answer with a full sentence: I intend to continue the hunger strike.

– I intend to continue their hunger strike until Grigorenko and Galanskov is released.

Everything was translated, I got my *svaboda Grigarjenka i Galanskov*.

– You are previously made aware that for the sake of your health we can not allow you to put your health at risk as long as you are in the Soviet area. Seeing as you do not voluntarily intend to resume normal food intake, the authorities consider it necessary to break the hunger strike by force. You still have the opportunity to reverse your decision.

He turned again to the trustee, who confirmed that I was given a new opportunity, which I rejected once more:

– I intend to continue my hunger strike.

What was now about to happen, I had no idea. How to cancel a hunger strike by force? I thought they would be waiting until the striker were halfway into a coma before they eventually added liquids by a tube, I figured a lot, and nourished some romantic notions of a Gandhi who appeased empires with his hunger and kept it going for years. But here they were short of time. My imperial thoughts were tiny and disappeared like bread crumbs on bird feeders, now I was a crumb on the feeder.

Warden Smirnoff and the trustee and the interpreter left the room. The physical pain does not need an interpreter. I should have read a bit more about the brave suffragettes, I should have learned how Lady Pankhurst had her throat blocked by clamps and liquid food fed directly into the body, I should perhaps have given up and had I known about the suffragettes' lonely hunger battle, I really might have.

Now it was too late. In came six men. They are huge they are employees, no fellow detainee – this is a job for professionals. A woman is standing in the background. Is it the doctor–lady or the Pirque–girl? I do not know, this will go down in a healthy fashion, they will not deprive me of more than my decency and nothing is life threatening.

Brutally I'm broken down on the bench. It is their brutality that make me resist, they intend to break the resistance before it comes, and I am panicking from all this power. I lie on my back but am still fighting, they do not really get a hold of me and the game hardens, they try to keep my head but no one will get my head and I am frantically jerking back and forth, my head is all I have for crying out loud! and they give up nailing me on he bench, it would have been better if they had asked me to be quiet but now they do something or other with me but I do not know what, and this unexpected pain is the worst of all pains and finally I'm lying on the floor.

I am overtaken. Taken over by six men, they sit on me, one on each arm and one on each foot and he who keeps my head do not intend to fondle with my hair and here comes the hose and is there a man on my chest, too? but maybe it's just the burden of unspeakable horror and nameless fear and a vice around my head, they will enter the hose through the mouth and where are all comfortable probes I have been dreaming about? in a different reality for here I am in the middle of my own precarious reality and it is filled up with a huge hose, it hovers in front of my eyes and parts into two, there are two hoses they will put into my body and I'm going to burst, what the hell are they doing, they really do not want to strangle me and I hold my breath in despair, will not open my mouth but now they squeeze my nostrils, I am almost blacking out, I do not give in, almost fainting but I do not give in and they can not possibly let me suffocate here and then what would happen to them? Would they have anything but prison camps to live in for the rest of their lives and then they give up.

Brief orders barked, they give up. I keep my mouth shut, they switch to the thinner tube and thus has not given up more than temporarily, they consider it risky to pour something into my stubborn throat and then chose another entrance: the nose. No one can close the nose. All sitting on post, all sitting on top of me. They have not read about the suffragettes, Pankhurst got a yoke around her jaws and thus escaped all resistance. Now they stick a tube through my nose. It is thick enough for me to lose my breath immediately, and my mouth pops up. Too late, they are on their way inside the tube through the nose. It stops at the glottis and I choke momentarily. I cannot swallow and I panic, a monster keeps a hold on my neck and I can not breathe, can not swallow and here comes a whole surge of a hot and sticky substance washing down my throat, it comes in through the nose, I cannot swallow away and I cannot close my throat and I am drowning, it is like water boarding, I am struggling and screaming and no sound is emitted apart from desperate bubbles bursting on the surface far above me, I'm on the ocean's depths and kicking free from a man, I'm about to drown and want to go up, up! And finally they stop and my stomach is a slimy bag with half of the ocean inboard and enough! I scream enough! Enough! Enough!

But they do not listen or they can hear me all too well, they do need their little revenge and here they start anew again, they have only eased the hose a little bit away but now it's in place, they have a big funnel at the other end of reality as we know it and they just ran out of what frightfully slush material they do fill me up with and here they start anew again, they pulled out the stopper and the entire ocean is surging into my lungs and pushing away the air and my wits and intelligence and I'm senseless, no more anxiety left for now I am drowning, here I lie helplessly alone with the whole ocean tapping at my lips and wanting so much to gush into my body all at once, and it is green, everything around me is green and the walls closing in on me, the roof sitting on my chest now and my fingers grasping desperately at some legs, it is a human leg and yet there is hope, there is a man down here in the depths of humiliation and abject fear, and suddenly I'm gone.

... and slowly faces are sliding back in front of me. I'm lying on the floor on my back on the bottom of a room, I have people around me and my lower parts are full of a sticky nasty liquid.

– Enough, enough! I scream. I give up, I give up, *stoj, stoj!*

A *stop* in Russian must help, I have proved my small heroism and I am left alive on the shore, I want my life back and the woman in tunic is nodding and there is indeed the interpreter, I wonder if she's been here the whole time you sadistic little fuck, but she is just stupid. She is just stupid and can't be of any help, she asks me in Norwegian:

– Do you intend to continue the hunger strike, or will you call it off? You must reply with a complete sentence.

– *I give up! Hunger strike is off, for the love of ... !*

All the fourteen guards are leaving, it must at least have been that many, I'm only just a fraction firmer than the porridge surrounding me and they almost have to tow me back to the cell.

They almost manage to close the door, before my body explodes. My stomach is growing, it was as small as a pointed bag and it has the full number of gallons of unspeakable stuff and the bag bursts. Like a balloon filled with water my stomach bursts and I just barely manage to knock at the door, sobbing *toilet basjalst* before I get choked again, it comes from within, the sea wants to get back in place and I can do nothing, there is tremendous powers within me and far too crowded, the whole Gulf of Finland is tearing at me and wants to go back in place, banks of fog already on the way out of my nose, Pyotr and the others understand what is going on, I've got the river Neva and the entire delta inside of me and it is surging beyond its banks, slowly trickling at first and cautious, a roar rises from my chest and a huge pillar brings down the bridges around, being the arms trying to help me, the warders pushing and towing and carrying me down to the toilet, we are making a narrow escape and a new explosion is on its way but heading out the other end this time, we give up the toilet on our way and they escort me straight into the shower, they know all too well that no man should be seen like this, they let me fall down on the wooden shutters on the floor, leaving the door standing open and there I lie, it's just my head that does not burst, but the rest of the body do, like an underwater volcano all my inside is bursting out both top and bottom.

Top and bottom without stopping.

For a long time I lie like this. I have let loose all that was inside of me, I'm in the midst of all this and never have I been nearer a toilet—like hell.

Quietly, Pyotr and the others enter. They do not utter a word. Gently gently removing all my clothing. Carefully they turn on all the showers. Pyotr measures the temperature of the water, it feels cool and comfortable for my body, so they leave me alone I'm lying there on my back and the water trickles around me and slowly slowly my life is turning back. Here my head is returning. Something loosens in there and I cry, I have no strength left to cry so I just let it cry, my head is crying at it's own pace, it is the rhythm of my heart that governs the tears and the water is everywhere and I sense with the tip of my tongue that some of the water is salty, it is my own salt and there is water inside and water outside and there is water everywhere and I am left on the beach.

After a while I get a towel. I get a real towel, a genuine terry towel and I do not bother to wonder where that one came from, it helped me rub my life back into a more familiar form, I get new a pajamas and a new dressing–gown, they smell fresh and clean and I got my hair washed and for sure I certainly got some shampoo? All warm and new, I was brought back to my room wondering whether it is cocoa tonight and freshly baked bread, as after my childhood's weekly baths on Fridays.

But I lie on the bed and have no strength left, they come with the evening meal and there they are all standing, a couple of the employed guards as well but none of them were involved in the disgracefulness, they are only called upon to testify that I am consuming again.

I eat. I chew three pieces of bread and two small spoons of cabbage and gasoline, it threatens to come back up immediately but I'm holding on, I'll never experience anything like this ever in my life, I hold on to what I have digested and a small sip of tea and sugar and then it stays down.

More ... I do not manage. They are satisfied, but they leave the door open for an hour or so as a precaution, we shall not have any covert hunger strikes around and what do they think I am? A hero? Far from it.

I'm just a useful idiot.

17

THE PROCESS

– *Choligansva!*

The man who says this is Semjon Semjonovitsj Haifetz, my defender. A little man in his early 50's, slender and intense. He told me that he was a Jew, he believed I would have gathered that much from his name. It didn't take him long time to get my confidence. But they said this much at the embassy: We will provide you with a defender who is fearless, who has defended dissidenters before almost pro bono. Trust him, he is clever. Currently, there is little more we can do to help you.

This was February the third 1970, it was a Tuesday, and I was on my way to what the Soviet author Alexandr Solshenitzyn called *The first Circle* (В круге первом, *Vi kruge pervom*). That book was published in the West in 1968, and was circled in the Soviet Union on *samizdat*, the underground press system. The reference is to Dante Aillighieri's *Divinia Comedia*, where the first circle is the first of nine – leading ultimately to Hell. The first circle is characterized as Limbo, which was exactly where I felt I was. The second circle, on the other hand, is Lust ...

Haifetz told me about the attention these demonstrations have attracted in the West, one was now expecting to present three cases before Soviet courts in quick succession. It seemed that mine was the first one. He confirmed the story of the three Italians, that they were three and not

106

two as Johannes believed, and also a Dutch student who had demonstrated in Kiev just before me. The last one I did not know about. – But since it seems that they raise charges against you first, they are planning to appoint you this year's prisoner ...

This year's prisoner! I was about to be appointed prisoner of the Year and how will I ever be able to achieve something greater than this currently peakest of peaks in my career?

– ... prisoner of the year by Amnesty International, the London branch. And again:

– *Choligansva!* said my defender,

– Cynical, malicious hooliganism, said the interpreter, and *hooliganism* in English was what a ruffian does, I thought, and now its troublemaker I am, a real hooligan. I was not so sure I liked that particular development, but Semjon Semjonovitsj Heifetz believed that such an accusation would make the trial a lot easier:

– But listen up. They do not want a political trial. Now they are obviously orchestrating a minor case of offences against public order, why in heaven's name do they take the burden of a public trial at all?

– Because the penalty is from one to 3 three years.

And there was a trial, I was accused of a traffic offence, I disobeyed the orders of my solicitor and quoted the "svoboda Grigorenko i Galanskov" from the leaflets that disturbed the traffic to a public that was remarkably polite and curious, and then it was time for sentencing.

The verdict:

– "Gjengset's actions are properly qualified as malicious mob behavior (choligansva, hooliganism) if the defendant with his conduct of exceedingly and aggravated cynicism had disturbed public order. Through distribution and exclamations, he gathered a crowd of people while expressing an insulting attitude to the Soviet people in his endeavor to evoke a hostile attitude to the Soviet state authorities as it is stated in the leaflets.

So it is determined Gjengset Gunnar's question of guilt that he has conducted evil behavior, completely proven by the above mentioned evidence. On the basis of the above mentioned judged Gunnar Gjengset, born this and that date to a year in prison. The sentence shall be served in Labor camp with strict regime."

One year in a Soviet prison camp, with strict regime. The journalists from the Western newspapers went to their offices and wrote their reports about this Norwegian creating all this brouhaha in the face of Brezhnev, the audience went to their homes and kept eating their cabbage soup. And later they turned on their television sets and watched the World Championships in figure skating, as the reporter Zubarev wrote in Leningradskaya Pravda:

"In the glare of the projector's light a young boy and a young girl slipped across the ice to the tune of Edvard Grieg. This magnificent spectacle could also have been watched by Gunnar Gjengset. He could have listened to his great compatriot's music. But at that moment Gjengset with sadness in his eyes regarded his father, who had temporarily left his law practice in Trondheim and was now on his way out of the already deserted courthouse in Tolmatsjev Street."

Three weeks passed. I had one meeting with Heifetz, then he was gone. He received an invitation from the Norwegian Board of Lawyers, but he never made it to Norway. He was gone, he had to set up practice in less central areas of the country. The only one that had to serve in this case was Semjon Semjonovitsj Heifetz, Russian lawyer and a Jew.

Back in my cell again, alone in the world. Weeks passed. Then the trustee arrived.

– You have a visitor, he said.

I strolled into the rest room for the guards on duty. There was a well–dressed man, he had an aura of travels about him but also of vodka, he was wearing a silk tie and a very relaxed smile. He was alone.

– Good evening, Mr. Djenset. I am Jegor Rakov. I am from the Foreign Ministry. Please sit down.

He spoke English easily and fluently, admittedly with a heavy Russian interference, but effortless. He came from the Foreign Ministry, and regretted that the appeal was dragging out.

– We are looking into some other possibilities. It might be easiest for everyone if you had admitted to having acted in error. The authorities only need a minor concession, so they might look with sympathy on solutions other than ... what shall we say, than the prison camp, the concentration camp.

And it sounded awesome dramatically in English, *concentration camp*, I was profoundly tired, down to the spinal cord and I was willing to admit to almost anything. The time for the great oblivion was beginning to approach, I asked a little more about what he had in mind and he sketched a tiny note where I stated that I was misinformed about the Soviet legal practice, that I therefore probably should have chosen another way to express my concern for certain Russian citizens, that I regretted and pardon me and I'll never do it again.

– We must put an end to this as soon as possible, he said looking rather busy, he had an appointment with the next cafe. He patted me encouragingly on the back, then he was gone again and I wondered – had he ever been there?

A few more days passed. I had put together some sweet little excuses that did not discredit anyone else but myself, I have realized that they intended to keep me here until I softened. They will not send me to an exciting labour camp, no Ivan Denisovitsch for me – they will leave me to wither in my own loneliness. So I was fabricating my small petition and it is night, it's time for brushing my teeth when into my cell the trustee came rushing:

– *Gjongset, Gjongset, Hjelsinki, nach Hjelsinki!* (to Helsinki!)

– Don't ridicule me, I said. – *Spaß nicht, bitte.*

But it was no joke. He had cleaned and pressured my suit, now he came up with a shaving machine and a pocket mirror, the warders gathered in the doorway and to their rhythmic clapping I shaved myself here in my cell in the Soviet Union. I did not need long time to pack. I put a pack of cigarettes in my pocket and bequeathed the rest of the stock to my benefactors, my fellow inmates who had made my life bearable. They might not know that, but anyone knows who has spent more than one day in isolation or as in my situation: double isolation – knows about the unbearable. Even that wall of double, linguistic isolation, they had helped me to take on, with Emil and his detectives in our pockets, we had scraped small holes in the language borders.

– *Gute Reise* and have a safe return, said Pyotr, *dasvedanja* (hope to see you again!)

– *Dovidinsja zaftra* I replied, see you tomorrow.

– *Sind Sie verheiratet*, he continued, (are You married?) and I answered as true was:

– *Da, u menja jest dotsj*, yes, I have a daughter and now it was just screams and laughter everywhere, it was a wistful congregation, and this is moments to remember in the middle of murky memories of this total abandonment. Suddenly there was Jegor, reeking of perfume and vodka, he asked me if I wrote that little … statement and I handed it over, I looked away rather embarrassed but have found out that nobody was interested in me anymore in the Western press, it was Saturday evening, February 21st and everyone had forgotten about me, they were sneaky enough to send me out in the middle of the weekend when all editors were off duty.

He glanced through my note, nodded and grunted a little, looked at me quite encouragingly and threw away the whole thing. I was terrified, he must have seen the lights go out in my eyes and he hurried on:

– No no, do not be afraid! It was only a matter of good will. Now let's move.

I took leave of Pyotr and the guys, I begged him never to steal radios no more and he gets the final line:

– *"Die Trip nach Berlin kann losgehen".*

– *Helsinki, basjalst!* I muttered, *Helsinki* – and we're gone.

Of course, the trial was far more dramatic, as was also my return from the Soviet Union – partly by train around the Karelia, in order to lead the Western press on a goose chase. But I got my fifteen minutes of fame; I was constantly on talk shows and stomaching barrels of liqueur without ever getting drunk. But suddenly it was all over, at last came the time for the great oblivion and I never got sober. Until now.

Gjengset dømt til ett års straffarbeide i Leningrad

Den norske student ble bl.a. kjent skyldig i «ondsinnet bråkmakeri»

Fra Aftenpostens medarbeider PER EGIL HEGGE
Leningrad, 9. februar.

Trondheim-studenten Gunnar Gjengset ble mandag dømt til ett års hardt straffarbeide for ondsinnet bråkmakeri. Han skal sone dommen i en arbeidsleir med strengt reglement. Soningstiden regnes fra 22. januar iår, da Gjengset ble arrestert på hovedgaten i Leningrad etter at han hadde delt ut brosjyrer med protester mot krenkelser av menneskerettighetene i Sovjet.

Retten fant at den norske student hadde utvist en «overordentlig» kynisme» ved at han grovt hadde krenket den offentlige orden og fornærmet sovjet-menneskers verdighet. Gjengset erklærte seg ikke skyldig efter tiltalen og hevdet at utdelingen av løpesedlene hadde vært en fredelig demonstrasjon. Maksimumsstraffen for «ondsinnet bråkmakeri» er fem års fengsel.

Aktor la ned påstand om to års

opphold i arbeidsleir. Forsvareren ville ikke «odta at «gjen horte inn under den paragraf Gjengset stod tiltalt for, og nedla påstand om botestraff og øyeblikkelig løslatelse. At Gjengset ble dømt til opphold i arbeidsleir med «strengt reglement» innebærer innskrenket adgang til å motta besøk og post, mindre matrasjoner og hardere arbeide.

Fortsatt side 14 **(4)**

Gunnar Gjengset.

Aftenposten 9th of February, Oslo 1970:
"Gjengset sentenced to one year of hard labour in Leningrad"

Part Two:

A DAY IN THE LIFE

18

LEAVING LAS VEGAS

– **Well. So much for** fearlessness. I will say adequately documented. Rather recklessness,

as Peter put it. He was referring to my tale of prison & punishment in another world, in another time. He interpreted my story as one about will: Specifically, if the conviction is a serious one, you can will yourself to endure duress, interrogations and even imprisonment. And in some situations one can will oneself not to eat. Therefore: Not to drink is a matter of will. *Just do it!*

Peter is an old friend from high school – I hadn't seen him for centuries. He had moved to Oslo, the capital of Norway, years ago. And now, so did I. And *now* was around 2005. Since 1970 I had established a family, made two children – a boy and a girl –, graduated with a master's in the science of literature, made some studies on literature for children and driving bus in the evenings and weekends, running half marathons whilst being sober half of the time.

Yes, and I divorced, lived together with different ladies, successively! worked as an assistant professor at different university colleges and conducted research on children and the medias at a university for several years. Then I flunked with my doctoral thesis. And always sober half of the time. But now I lost my footing. So once again I fled, to Oslo this time. Trying never to get sober.

Peter was trying to grasp my reasoning around why and how I ended up at the bottom of a bottle. It wasn't easy, because I never really let go – I was always busy doing other things. Such as writing out the partial diary from my Soviet campaign, based on the scraps of paper and scraps of memories, into some sort of a book.

– You'll never succeed in becoming a full–fledged drunkard with your range of activities, he commented.

– Just you wait. For the time being I'm just fooling you. What you don't see, is my successful pattern: When I go out for a beer, that beer will last me five days. The last two days I'm back in job, but only partially. When the next weekend comes, I'm all set. Which means that I am drunk half the year, roughly. Or half of my life, to put it that way. Hardly a professional drinker, am I?

– How professional can you get?

– The Real Thing is drinking around the clock until you drop.

– The Leaving Las Vegas thing?

– The Leaving Las Vegas thing. Never let go of the glass. A conscious suicide...

– ... only the gang actually practicing The Real Thing...

– ... ain't conscious.

– But you are, concluded Peter.

– But I am, conceded I.

He shrugged.

– But you also mentioned another book when you stumbled in here some time, easily refreshed. A biography of Matti Aiko ...

... Aikio!

– Okay. Aikio. Sami writer, you said. Are you a Sami?

– No. I have never managed to find a single small tip of a Sami brogue in my family, who rather descended from Norwegian travelers.

– Anyway, you wrote a biography of a Sami writer?

– Pure laziness.

– How come?

– Because I had already written a dissertation for a Master's degree on him. The reason that I chose Aikio was that it was almost not written a word about him from before. Imagine having to write about Ibsen, there are several miles of books about him! Pure madness, of course.

– And you are of course not as cynical as you pretend. Have you lived in Finnmark, perhaps?

– For one year, as a teacher.

– First student, then a clerk in a bookstore, a teacher, something with running a hotel ...

– ... and you can feel free to add bus– and truck driver, milkman, delivering newspapers, janitor, car shop mechanic, managing the sports department in a hypermarket, stock consultant on handling rail freight, fish monger and fillet cutter, chef and stoker at the brickworks ... But gondolier I've never been.

– Gondolier?

– A man who rowed people in a rowboat across the canals of Trondheim. I have always wanted a rowboat for myself.

– Then I ask you straight out: Have you been at sea? I mean, as a sailor?

– Wow, did I forget that? I shipped with S/S *Stavangerfjord* in 1962, sailed during my summer holidays from Oslo via Copenhagen to New York, two weeks each way, until I graduated from high school in 1965, when I took an extended trip through the Panama canal, up along the west coast to Canada and back, the M/S *Burrard*, a freighter with twelve passengers. I advanced to second chef there...

– That's what I was hoping for, Peter said teasingly.

– This is actually a major indication of ADD. Those who did not manage to sit still, or didn't succeed at school, were those most likely to go to sea.

– It is reasonable, but I have not thought of it. And it doesn't fit: I was always a smart pupil, and now and then too smart for my own good. But I have a friend, my best man actually, he has ADD and drank and partied and sailed for the West Indies in his youth. Now he is a drained up lawyer with a big tattoo. We joke about the bad old days.

Peter the reader was lecturing me:

– In the 1950's, one diagnosed hyperactive boys that reacted positively to Ritalin as suffering from ADD. Those were the same youngsters who went to sea immediately after graduation, the fifteen–year–olds.

– I was fifteen and a half. Then I met another criterion, perhaps?

– Definitely, but what did you really do in Finnmark?

– I began to drink. That is, I had drunk for a long time, of course, but not been *drinking* – if you know what I mean. Even before I turned sixteen, I was drunk for the first time. But that was a setup, at Charlie Bar in New York, during my maiden voyage aboard the SS Stavangerfjord. The nearest bar in the port area is always called Charlie Bar. I was sick, miserable and seriously scared: wooden floors of the warehouse were doing the most extraordinary maneuvers to slap me on my forehead, and it was with great difficulty that I vacillated myself on board again. Since that incident there was the two to three beers behind the barn every Saturday while I was in high school, but throughout the period we were busy celebrating High School Graduation, I was soaking sober! I was dating a daughter of a famous teetotaler in Trondheim, but she did not even notice that I did not drink, because she did not herself drink, either. She was also partly engaged, and the engagement continued into matrimony right after the celebrations, so my temperance was completely wasted. Besides, I was a little engaged myself with a girl one class below me at school and we exchanged rings the following year.

– Alcohol was not important, in other words?

– Not to start with. But I had a couple of sensual meetings alone with Brother Alcohol. Once I had the house of my girlfriend all to myself for a weekend, we had got engaged after her graduation in 1966. This must have been the next year; perhaps I was home on leave – from the navy? In any case, I sat alone all weekend and listened to the Beatles' *Sgt. Pepper's Lonely Hearts Club Band*. That title! There I sat with my lonely heart and listened to a whole band of lonely hearts, I listened to him that fixed a hole where the rain came in, and thought that was what I wanted to do for the rest of my life, I was fox hunting around the living room, read the news about four thousand holes in Blackburn, Lancashire along with John Lennon and was happy. I was bobbing along all by myself, felt rather blessed and drank claret. Red wine in and my wits out, while I pondered on the strange message of *Within You Without You*. I went nowhere and drank with no one, and it gave me a deep sense of satisfaction. Maybe I was back in the kayak of my childhood, maybe I was in a rowboat with my father, who was every moment just on the brink of breaking out into a sentence or two for me, for just me and nobody else in the world, and the world swayed lazily around me, the sun was warm and round up in the sky somewhere and slowly it trickled down into my stomach. There is sun in each bottle, the Beatles sang, the warmth rose within me and my ears were carefully caressed by this wonderful music with this strange message that *grows so incredibly high,* and this was happiness, this was happiness and happiness was all that was sloshing, all that bobbed, happiness was red wine and loneliness.

    – A dangerous illusion, Peter said.

    – A lovely illusion.

19

HOW NOT TO DRINK

Later I learned more about loneliness and absence, and about drinking: It gives me the happiness of not drowning, of not dying, even if I undergo death every single time. Drinking gives hopes of happiness, but anticipations of death.

– What was bothering you?

– Everything that was going on around me, I think. If I ran away, I was followed by the turmoil. It grew, and drove me out on the road. So I started training for competitions! I ran and ran, and it gave me a kind of transient intoxication. I have always had a good relationship with my endorphins. Hashish I have tried, it is good for digestion, and you can even listen to the music with your stomach! But otherwise? LSD took me on a fantastic trip one summer I lived alone in the countryside, and the nature there was never the same. Still, I can take my hand slowly in front of my eyes and see it in slow motion, played out in slow picture frames. Never again! Then I'm guaranteed a bad trip.

– Let's stick to the alcohol. Does it also give you bad trips?

– No, with alcohol any trip is a rally. Happiness is anything sloshing, and after a time one is crawling for anything sloshing, if only the last little sip on the bottle, and if there is no more, you get an accident, as they put it up north. Not to say that I began to repair, but from then on the only reason to drink was to get drunk. Drinking was a tour de force, the total annihilation. Or the gradual drowning, if you will.

– And you already understood that?

– By no means. Something like that I would never admit. The fact was that I got loaded each time I touched a beer, that I was exercising only so I could visit the pub with the guys on the relay team every Friday. Strangely enough the team also introduced quick pub–visits on Saturdays, or at least that was what I told my wife. Obviously none of my team–partners knew anything about these Saturday meetings. But I still did not drink, I trained for chrissake, I even ran a half marathon! I ran and ran until one asked me what I was running from? I had to answer for myself that it was my wife I was running from. But it did not have to be true, maybe I only ran from her as my guardian, she nagged and nagged about the drinking. But I earned twice as much as she did, didn't I? Did I not write books and articles, and songs and shows in all this turmoil, and who was it that bought all the furnishings with money earned from bus driving, as I had done all through my student days? So I ran and drank and drank and ran, but then along came this therapist and what are you running from he asked, and I stopped abruptly. Since then I have never ran needlessly. But my physical condition is in good shape; therefore, I can drink more. And therefore conserve myself better.

– It almost sounds like an aphorism. But your job suffered?

– Only rarely, because I worked rather short hours. I have never understood this talk about preparing for hours for a simple lecture, or those who use days to correct a bunch of compositions. It's done in a wink, as we say.

– For you to have some more time to drink?

– For me … no, I really didn't think like that. I have always used the time needed to accomplish my work. Neither more nor less. It's not my fault that there is too much time in the world! I have plenty of time to spare!

– And that may be the problem? Peter wondered.

– But I was like drinking every Wednesday and Friday and Saturday, and maybe a little beer for dinner on Sunday and I had some small bottles hidden away. Anyone recognizing a pattern here? Not me, certainly.

– And the reason?

– I was overtaken. As an adult with an education, after I had been fooling around for a considerable time, some of it spent in Russia by the way... But when I started a family, I was overtaken. I worked two years as an assistant professor, and already I started to lose the grip. It was not true that the employment council of that university college was on to me, as I have told you before, it was rather me starting to make myself impossible for further employment. One more year, and I would be able to claim a permanent position. My treacherous sub consciousness of course knew that it had to make me trip, for regular work is an impossibility! Besides, I had been with my wife for more than six years, and time was up three years ago, at least. My own childhood was finally over, adulthood was waiting outside my door. That is to say, the real adult life stood threateningly *inside* the door of our house, and the only way out was an escape. It lasted for nearly twenty years.

– What started it?

– I separated my wife and ran away from Tromso. But one cannot run away from one's childhood.

– Where did you go?

– To another small town further south with a university college, and I've probably already mentioned it, if you remember. A small town is never a cheerful place to be alone in. I taught literature at the college. There I discovered a serious deficiency in myself: I get easily tired of routines. This was my third year in the teaching business, and I could not comprehend how my more experienced colleagues were able to continue year in and year out. Now I had done the same job for three years, and it could not possibly be the meaning of life that I should continue indefinitely with this line of work. Should I stand in front of a blackboard and lecture about folk songs and fairy tales for ten years, twenty, thirty ....? I hate routines, and those were a little tiring for someone who indulged in the most routine-based vice of all, namely drinking.

– But wouldn't you rather talk about the work?

– Actually, I have had the same experience with almost all the jobs I have ever had: When I learn my job fully, it appears inconceivable to me that I should continue with that job for the rest of my life. What's the point? Here I have got one lifetime, and I shall spend it on ... teaching rhymin' cockney? Year after bloody year? I'd rather drive a bus! I would go crazy, and one day I would walk on the wall instead of through the front door.

– Or *Through The Looking Glass*?

– Ha! You have read Charles Lutwidge Dodgson ...

– ...or Lewis Carroll and *Alice in Wonderland* ...

– *Alice's **Adventures** in Wonderland*, actually. Suggesting that one can visit alternating versions of the so–called reality. The Disney version states that you have to make a choice. And thus Disney ditched fantasy. Just ask the caterpillar! The ultimate book of my childhood.

– Spoken by a compassionate researcher. But you probably had the opportunity for research, Peter inquired.

– The question is rather what's the most dullest, yes. Research is not exactly hilarious. Which was my relationship with alcohol. Hilarious, that is ... From the northern regions I had brought with me some twisted nerves and a referral to a psychologist. But after two hours of conversation the *psychiatrist* declared that he could not help me. He admitted that he was fascinated by my stories, but claimed he would probably fail to maintain professional distance from me as a case. There went my last respect for science, at least psychiatry. He gave me a sick leave and a prescription for Valium, which I washed down with vodka. The Valium ... It is the most comfortable intoxication I've ever experienced, and I could have remained there for the rest of my life, that would have ended very quickly and uncomfortably. But I quit this polydrug abuse quite suddenly, for I realized that this was pure suicide.

And I was, and is not, suicidal. Therefore, out with Valium, out with psychiatrists, here I had to stand on my own feet.

– Your own sober feet?

– Well. I wasn't going to exaggerate. There followed some very drunken years. Because I had family in nearby Trondheim, the school administration friendly enough put me up with teaching only on the middle three days of the week. I thus got unusual oval weekends. But I never went to Trondheim, and all that time I spent with my best friends Nick Teen and Al K. Hall.

I started drinking after school on Thursday, then twenty–four–seven until Sunday evening, but then I stopped. Trembled and sweated my way through Monday, and was ready for a new week on Tuesday.

– Sure, so you learned to drink properly in that town?

– I became a drink fundamentalist. I asked no questions, but swallowed away. Mostly at some cafe, for still I was only an apprentice. It would be even worse the following year when I moved to Trondheim and started working at the Cathedral's High School. That was in the fall of 1983, I maintained the separation and now we began quarreling about child custody. We had rounds of hearings and observation by psychologists.

– Because you drank?

– I still did not drink, not *really*. The drinker is totally and ruthlessly unreliable about his drinking. Once it was a miracle that the appointed psychologist did not notice that I had been drinking. I pulled myself sharply together, and it was always neat and tidy at home. My son was happy and satisfied, and played actively with the boys in the street. No need to worry. But the psychologist never saw the times my son and I had been out eating pizza, when I usually had a bottle of wine or two, and also had a couple of bottles hidden at home.

Or the times I chewed coffee beans when I picked my son up at school, or called and asked if he possibly could walk home alone by himself, I had a troubled back.

Or the times I tried to make him buy beer for me at the grocery store, showing them a note from the father. Or ... But someone at school noticed what really was going on of course, and the school's supervisory physician received a disturbing message.

– How did you respond to that?

– I never worried about such messages. They were totally unfounded, of course.

– Of course.

– But my son must have noticed the few times we took the wrong bus from the city, for example, and ended up far out in suburbia and father did not quite know how to get home. Or Saturday noons, when we sat for hours on dubious pubs with some friends, and where he ultimately refused to enter, on the grounds that he hated the smoke from cigarettes.

– Children are quick to rewrite reality, to not offend their parents, you know.

– But finally he couldn't take it anymore. He wanted to move back to his mother's – although because he claimed to miss his sister ... that little bugger! I did not hesitate, but rallied him immediately back to his mother. That put an end to the hostilities from his mother.

– I thought so myself, yes. What you do not take into account is that now you could drink in peace. Said Peter.

– Maybe, but it was my son's call, and it was not an easy one. But now I could drink what I wanted, if I just kept sober on the job. I had merely an engagement at the Cathedral's college. Norway has got just one Cathedral, you know, so the position was rather prestigious. It was not always that easy, and there was mornings when I had to throw down a pint in a doorway before I dared to enter the class. In a way the job was OK, my students at the Cathedral did like me, strangely enough, it was perhaps because no curriculum was sacred to me. And for one entire year I put up with that job. And I have to admit that the reason I put up with this rather tedious teaching routines, was the pupils: They were recruited from groups of teenagers that were from endangered milieus: Youngsters that actually were looking for work in times of unemployment – this initiative was a deployment of kids who otherwise would be on the dole.

– Outsiders, so to speak?

– Outsiders, and I immediately felt at home ...

– ... as you feel amongst emigrants, indigenious, drunkards ...

– ... and other outcasts! For sure. A splendid year, actually. We felt we were soul mates. And I moved to a smaller flat nearby. But the next year I was invited into the Headquarters of the Cathedral school, with all it's posh founders and renowned head masters and ...

– ... the whole shabang of conservative schooling? – Exactly. How could I dare to face this peace of reality in a sober way?

– Abandoned by your son, stuck with a job you hated, your mind filled with captivating matters ...

– I was heading for the first circle.

20

THE FIST CIRCLE: A DRUNKARD'S MESSY ROUTINES

– **Worse rounds I had** with a psychologist I had started to frequent. He asked me to tell him about my drinking, and I told him the truth, that drinking was not a problem. But **tell** me, he insisted. And I told him. About how I crashed on the pub right after school every Friday, albeit after having bunkered up properly at home: wine for two days, and beer enough for careful repairs on Sunday. Then nothing for the rest of the week, but Monday started with some serious yelling and bellowing in the great phone. Well, maybe it was a beer or two on Wednesday, it could also happen that I stopped by for a drink on Thursday, and then it was the weekend, right? Everybody was drinking during weekends. I was always the last one to leave for home, and I never went home without making sure I had stored some more there. To drink. I couldn't go to bed sober either, I was free from job the day after.

The psychologist seemed to be impressed, claiming that I could really drink and ironically added that I ought not end that. I was in control, he argued. But then he asked the difficult question.

– What was it? Peter was obviously collegially curious.

– How did I think it was going to turn out, once I was alone? As if he knew that I was lonely always, but I was not fucking alone. I had a girlfriend again.

– So you were in control, Peter said rhetorically, but why do you really drink?

– Because quietness is slowly spreading in my head, I replied, I can only bob away and no one can catch me. And the drinker can fool everyone for a long time, but never himself, not deep down. And if it is Skid Row you are heading for, you will get there.

– Drinking is a slow suicide, Peter insisted, and was of course quite right. So I told him how it goes down:

– It takes a week to get sober after a decent drunk spree, which for me lasts up to five days. Rarely more. For I quit drinking when I can't bear it anymore, and it may well happen in the middle of a glass. It's always beer and wine left in the house, but when I stop, it's full stop. After all, I am a habitual smoker who never smokes more than three cigarettes per day. When I drink, the amount increases up to ten. No more.

At the same time order crumbles around me; newspapers pile up, dirty dishes, full ashtrays and empty bottles, and this is heavy for the Master of Neatness. And I'm crash–landing in the same routine hell every time, in spite of my fear of procedures.

– How do these routines look like? Peter asked.

– First, vomiting, – lasting long after it's anything left to throw up. But at 12:00 noon on the first day it ends. Then I drink pools of water, trying to smoke, permanently sick, can't stomach anything and unable to sleep for a second the next night. But it does not matter, because I have not been able to read newspapers for the days I was being besotted, so I line them up after dates, and read every word. The night passes, but the diarrhea stays.

– And day two?

– I finally manage to keep my food. A little cautious at first, sweating over every one bit. Besides, I'm very tender towards all kinds of impressions, especially sounds and light. It people on the street are closing up on me a little abruptly, I jump several meters. I am terribly irritable, and all messages on radio and television are loudly commented. If there is an argument, I am quickly taking leave of my senses. Then comes the night again, but not sleep. The third day is more or less as day two, but now I am also fundamentally tired. Maybe I'm napping in my chair, but usually I'm hyperactive, my legs keep walking while my head does not know where I'm heading. I keep wandering restlessly about.

– And what's next?

– The fourth day is the worst. Tiny hallucinations lurking in the corner of my eye, I'm so tired of insomnia that I start cringing for the smallest matter. I read in the paper about a stray kitten, I immediately shed a tear. But my inner crocodile is laughing his evil laughter. This day is also miraculously coming to an end, aided by videos. Another sleepless night is awaiting, but maybe sleep sneaks in, and then guaranteed with a nightmare. Always the same one, filled with dogs, and they are big and dangerous. There are also children. They look very adult. Sullen, without a smile, eyes without a glow. The children begin to become aggressive, they bother me, also physically, and the dogs are helping them. They start nipping at me, baring their greedy jaws, froth gushing from them, they bite me and the kids are holding around my legs to keep me there, to make me fall so that the dogs really can get a bite, but before the first dog gets his tooth in my nose, I wake up gasping. Then it's all over. Trembling I stand up and make myself a cup of tea, swear that I will never drink again, knowing that this promise won't last long enough for anything. No sweat, a small nightmare I will probably always outlive. And thus life turns into a nightmare.

– But at that time, didn't a shrink specifically advice against drinking?

– I should stop drinking, he said, not forever, just for one year. After that I could drink as much as I would, because then I would be in complete control. Provided that I kept a teetotal regime for one entire year. With absolutely nothing to drink: NADA. NJETA. I replied sure, no big deal. Stop drinking a challenge for me who almost did not drink? But it got at me anyway, and I asked a good friend who had also had a pint or two in his life. He had kept sober for a year, and told me a story that I seemed to recognize. Namely: the job began to slip. He heard the whisperings in the corners, and so he quit. I mean drinking. The immediate effect was that he became totally friendless. He only knew people who drank, and you can't for very long ask for one *sin alcohol* for me, please. In public.

That is, your peers can't stand it. For strangely enough Mr. Temperance is perceived as a spy. You shall leave their drinking alone, and we want no one sober making notes of what we are downing! Old comrades are getting directly hostile after the third beer, and by that time you have already lost the interest in sitting there anyway. I mean, how exciting can it be to listen to people having sunk three pints, when one is sober oneself.

– But you persevered?

– I like to believe that. But it must have been worse. A short period of my life lies in semidarkness. It is something I have forgotten. And that's bad, because I never have blackouts. Never!

– What happened?

– For some reason I once ended up in the neurological department of the hospital, where they conducted both EEG test and a lengthy psychological test on me. The only explanation they gave me for being there, was that I had hyperventilated. But I had stopped doing that! Thinking back, a friend of mine had not brought me a couple of valiums, as I had requested – on the contrary, apparently I had called him after having swallowed a tray or two of Valiums, so maybe I had been rushed in for pumping? At least he told me afterwards that a couple of trays with Valium was nothing for us guys, but if I already was under the influence, that was something else. Hence the pumping.

– Possibly, but that would probably count as a suicide attempt?

– Yes, and I do not do suicides.

– Funny: I do not do suicides!

– Laugh your lungs out. Perhaps it was a so–called breakdown. I have only feeble recollections about the incident. The immediate explanation might have been the indomitable turmoil I always knew, and a permanent feeling that something was wrong with me.

– This was the late 1980's, right? At that time, hyperactives were not seen as more than just very active, and it's always positive to be active. So they probably had nothing to offer, other than sedatives.

– Something like that, and chemicals of that sort, I have always steered away from. For in the midst of all the turmoil, there is also a certain creek of creativity, you've already notified that, and I would rather not lose those faculties.

– As long as creativity is not exchanged for criminal acts, society at that time had nothing to offer the hyperactives, Peter agreed.

– But suddenly I ended up at the Regional Hospital, the neurological department. Where I told them about my frequent hyperventilation experiences some time ago, and so they checked me for epilepsy. They attached all sorts of things to my head, and drove me through various disco shows, but I reacted as healthy people do. In came a psychologist with an MIT–test, a questionnaire with more than hundred stupid questions. The test is developed at the Massachusetts Institute of Technology, and the intention was to reveal any sexual deviation, I learned afterwards.

– Not a suitable test for you, I think.

– Now I had undergone this test before, in the military service, and I passed. So I tried to read through the test with fresh eyes this time, since they used it on civilians as well. But I found out that the precision level was very low, the questions were too repetitive, and test developers surely must see that they had asked almost the same question several times before? So I offered the psychologist a proofreading, I could read through the test for him and weed out all double questions and imprecise formulations. The psychologist thanked me politely, and looked a little surprised. But I was free to leave, as sound and healthy, by the way.

– It is perhaps one out of 10 000 who would reply like that, Peter said.

– But I felt quite proud, and also somewhat stupid. What had I done wrong?

– Nothing. But the test is not intended for neurotics like you. It does in fact aim to uncover any sexual deviation, or preferences, which may be hidden from the client himself. As you have already mentioned. Therefore, one tries to fool the test subject by posing the same question several times, so that the client should be a little off guard, and thereby reveal themselves. But how wonderful was life outside of the tests?

– At this time I had moved to a small apartment and had been called by the Norwegian Centre for Child Research. It was just the place for me, who never really grew up. My analysis of famous iconic children's books and other literature finally gave me some credit. I had two years' leave of absence from my position at the Cathedral's High School for conducting research on children's reading habits. It evolved into studies on the children's media habits, based on the full range of leisure pursuits.

– How did you conduct your drinking under such conditions?

– Now, I was in for drinking in a really large scale. Of course I did not reason like that. Just like the professional drunkards' slogan goes: A case of beer just passed by. At the same time it was in and out with my girlfriend, literally. We tried to live together, until she threw me out. In that relationship I got all the rejection I could wish for.

– On the other hand, one could get the impression that you were trying out her limits: How much could you drink before she could not take it any more?

Peter is dangerously good, and he's obviously right:

– Exactly. I used that strategy with great success on several women, and it always ended with them saying thank you for the dance.

I do not want to ponder much upon this relationship, the whole adventure was an unhappy sidetrack which cost me so much misfortune that I barely endured. So finally, she left me.

21

HOW TO QUIT QUITTING

– **Last time we spoke** you would stage what you called your last great passage. Where did it take you? Peter said.

– To Oslo, I replied.

– Because of my research on children's literature, and especially for my critical articles about one iconic author ....

– Let's continue with the Oslo angle now, Peter interrupted.

– It was an escape, which I'm so good at, while nothing tied me to Trondheim longer: I had flunked in love and science that last year. You know ... my PhD–thesis bounced, and so did my girlfriend. At the same time the thesis version number two finally was cleared for submission, with assurances that it was almost impossible to be rejected. I was far from secure, I had already been rejected once. And I do have an unparalleled record in being rejected ...

– ... rejection being among your strongest disciplines, Peter said.

– Yes, definitely.

– Did you feel at home in Oslo?

– I soon found my regular cafe nearby. And since I had begun to pay my bills, I found out that I was rather deep in debts. Full of enthusiasm but empty on assets, I should start teaching after seven – eight years of research.

– How did that turn out?

– It was a shock.

– Because?

– The students at the University College of Oslo had one clear message for me: Could I please tell them how they should line up lessons in Norwegian for pupils in let's say the fourth grade. I tried to protest, said that it just was not my job.

– How did that play out?

– It ended with the students' complaint about my teaching. I had never dreamed that I would miss the turbulent 1970's with student's riots worldwide ... And since the students were not interested in what I had to offer, I did not even need one year to lose interest. It took only three weeks. Thus, it became an insurmountable yoke to attend classes. I was reluctant to go to work, and I dreaded returning home. Life at the College was completely pointless, and I perceived the students as downright enemies. They expected something of me that I could not give them, while I had something to offer that they were not interested in. And although my academic production got me a promotion as assistant professor, I took a sick leave. Then I might as well have a reason: I got so drunk that I lost my feet. I was completely spineless.

– In other words: You lost your footing.

– It can safely be put that way. It went well for quite some time, but very soon I spent the vacant hours in a pub just down the street from the college. Often I had lived through a couple of hours with much opposition, and was so frightened that I wanted to go home. I dared not meet people any more. I most certainly had some reason to feel guilty. For example, I had given up teaching literature, now I let the students mostly work on their own, sit in groups and then providing them with some inane "analysis" in which they restored the plot of the book. After all, that was what they wanted.

– But what would you want to do?

– Nothing at all. I was just sloshing off. At the end of the day, as one says, I went home. That's pure bragging, for on my way home, there is for example the waterhole called Schroeder. And then there was the little Indian shop with a bar a bit closer to home, and finally the Chinese restaurant around the corner from where I lived. I got that far around the time common people started returning from work. Those who teach at colleges, have an incredible amount of vacant time. In return, they earn unimaginable heaps of money to fill all this free time with, and therefore I almost never had to be sober. In such a life it certainly is a disadvantage to work faster than most others. And then something went so horribly wrong. I showed up drunk at school.

– Why didn't you just call in sick?

– Probably because I was too drunk to speak clearly, or simply too wasted to dial the number. In any case, too drunk to think, and I were rescued by a couple of attentive students who for some time had noticed that I had my own worries.

– What did they do?

– They took me friendly but firmly aside, got a car, canceled classes and notified the management of the school that I had left classes because of an ailment. Saved just before knockout! And the big paradox in all this, I was rescued by a resolute appearance of these hopeless students. I was the most hopeless one, oh yes!

– But the management had thoughts about this ... ailment, perhaps?

– Certainly. Although the management formally supported me, they probably thought that there must be fire somewhere since they could almost see the smoke. So I pulled myself together. Hell, I had been told that I would get a permanent job here, if only I would fit in. Many of my colleagues would have killed for such a job at this college. And I was gambling with such a possibility at stake?

– But gambling you were?

– Of course I would mess up such an opportunity. I was more than terrified by such a possibility: Regular work, in, out, out, in every single day with Ibsen and Pippi Longstockings? I knew that I did not have that many options, since I had already written off a doctoral degree. The choice was once again: A job or the gutter. The choice aroused a terrible anxiety, for I knew how cold it was in the gutter. But in many ways it was preferable...

– Now don't be silly, Peter interrupted.

– I said so myself, exhorted myself and went off to the teaching, scared to sobriety. But there, among the students, the inspector of the school was sitting. I made it clear that under such circumstances I could not teach. I could not work, if the management so doubted that I was able to do the job right that they had to have an inspector present. So I went home, this time for good. It was nearing Christmas, in the year of 1994. I carried home as much alcohol as I could manage to carry, locked the door and pulled out the phone. I told the kids that I would be away for a week, which in itself was true. After a few days there was someone at the door. I heard that it was the inspector and the Dean, they came to my home to check what I was doing! I got angry, but afterwards it struck me that perhaps they just wanted to check *how* I was doing.

I was getting almost sober on Boxing Day. The void after such a period is just about unbearable. It's not like the body is crying out for alcohol, it is crying out of pain. The entire machinery is totally busted, but at the same time we know that a beer or three will mitigate all the turmoil. Therefore, it is called to repair. It means to delay the problems for the next day, but we know that the symptoms will never go away, not until you stop.

– Nice of you to explain this to me, said Peter, rather sarcastic.

– You're welcome. For me it is a fixed pattern that after a complete ball, accumulated feelings strikes back with full force: All of a sudden I have a bunch of ideas of things that can be written, some ideas for a play, maybe a book about ... For example Thundershield, the Naval Hero? And at least two feature articles, now and then I wrote them and sent them to editors. To my horror, sometimes they were put on. And always I kept long complicated speeches for myself, I was planning new associations or political parties, and perhaps I should make a Hyde Park–cloning at Groenland, the Greenwich Village of Oslo? Stand up on a crate at a corner and give a brimstone sermon? And my head was getting so hectic that the best thing would be a beer to calm it all down ...

– But you didn't? You stopped?

– Everyone quits every now and then – or for good. Or like me: In the middle of a glass.

– I am a bit impressed with just that, Peter said. – You are therefore something as rare as a drunkard and a temperance man. But now you quit drinking, if I understand you correctly?

– Quite the contrary. I quit *quitting*. Previously, I had at least stopped once a week, but now I was looking at my life's last voyage. That I understood, but I could not decide whether I should choose the gutter or pursue some serious compromises in a job that I hated.

– You had really come to an end, and you felt that there was nowhere to hide?

– That's right. The situation was well known: I was standing outside a small neat house and peered into the small nice family who did nice things to each other, while I knew I would never be welcome. I am different! If I continued to drink now, it was my own fault, and I would remain an outsider forever. But if I stopped drinking, it was for my children's sake. In the middle of the glass, I stopped. But no, it's never *that* heroic for us abusers. I always used to drag home a lot of alcohol before I quit – better safe than sorry. But I stopped, no matter how much beer was left in the closet. I learned that I could stop if I wanted to. However, I had not learned not to start. My drinking has almost something cheerful about it: I reduce my activity into sheer routines and illness, and my fastidiousness collapses.

– For a meticulous man who hates disease and procedures, it is highly surprising that you completely wholeheartedly are self–producing your own distorted image.

– Completely voluntarily! Almost cheerfully.

– How does this ... cheerfulness appear?

– It begins with some wild bags of wine. Then follows pallets of beer, and then it all levels out. The last couple of days it is enough with three to four pints, and then it suddenly ends.

– You have told me that you are not suicidal, Peter asserted.

– Never. But at the same time I had this craving somewhere inside my belly, a lump that was aching in the stomach somewhere. It felt like a constant voltage, such as before exposing oneself for an oral exam. It was like this all the time, day out and day in, from the first slice of bread in the morning. Always this craving, this tension.

– Did you try to get help?

– I did. First I went to the man who was supposed to be my doctor. Why don't you just stop drinking, he reported – but ten years premature. He was not willing to try to get me an appointment with a psychologist either. Why did I need a psychologist? There was nothing special about me, he concluded after seven and a half minute consultation.

– What about your job?

– The year at college came to an end, and so did my doctoral dreams. I flunked. Again, I had counteracted myself, I think.

– I believe so too, Peter nodded.

– If you could restate the thesis, you would have succeeded with something in your life. That wouldn't harmonize with your discordant self–esteem.

– Right. My engagement at the University College was not extended. I had the rather unreasonable luck not to be fired. I barely avoided the gutter this time also. I still wrote my aphorisms for that paper, and therefore an estimated publishing house called me: If I could translate some proverb from Danish and Swedish for them? He thought I had the language that was needed. I translated a major Proverbs Encyclopedia, it was inspiring work and astonishingly well paid.

– You became a translator then?

– Exactly, and it was fixed translations for several years; I had commissions for Bang & Olufsen, Microsoft, and Apple. I even made commercials, sold the last bit of my soul, and

suddenly one day a branding company called Customer & Co flew me in on business class to Copenhagen. There, I participated in a brainstorming for a campaign for Bang & Olufsen's new speakers, along with the big boys from all over Europe.

– A hectic life, in other words?

– Amongst a crowd that flickered vigorously with fat credit cards and stiff drinks. But what they were doing was in my opinion crazy bull, and back home, I could quickly sink my murky future of overpaid advertising lies. I messed up with a prewritten text that I was responsible for, so it never reached the main office in Copenhagen. I was just as happy. A familiar feeling: As happy.

– But I thought you had stopped drinking, Peter said, surprised.

– Although I had more control over my drinking, the craving never quite disappeared. Not necessarily always craving alcohol, but rather *extinction*, or better: Withdrawal.

– A psychologist would call it retardation.

– The basic mood in my life is rejection and loneliness. If I'm met with success, I am drawn back there. Only alcohol creates that sounds of silence in my head, and brings peace to my permanent unrest.

– But how are you emotionally when you drink?

– Neither in these times do I really feel good, nor is it nice for others to be near me. I am harmless, but infinitely sad. Then I just sit and drink and keep staring out into thin air.

– Drinking is no solution, and there is no solution to stop drinking, you think?

– Rather that my demons never completely leave me no matter what I do, but I can try to ignore them.

22

THE ART OF
NOT TO START

– **I was a man who** ran amok. My efforts as a researcher had crashed, but I could do something very few scholars can: Create at least one aphorism per day. Some call it art...

– Wandering away from drinking, are we?

Peter can be such a prick.

– If one realizes that drinking is a problem, one can also solve it. Therefore we can pull ourselves together in relation to others, I suggest.

– It applies for all types of conditions, agreed Peter. – At work, with friends, family and even in the company with children.

– Although we feel bored, it is not necessary to demonstrate that to the entire world!

– Yes, exactly. It is important to talk football with the guys, if you hate football ever so much. It is important to listen genuinely and interestedly when your loved one brings you stories from work, even if it bores you. But the bored one is risking being alone with his boredom. And that is boring!

– When it comes to our own children, it is our utmost duty to be present. All the time! Then we do not rev up, do not bring the children into a cafe or other scary places to humor our own needs, we must rather face all the boredom that companionship with children is bringing.

The hardest exercise is presence, I concluded.

– Funny you should mention it, because I was just getting there. When you are busy fighting all sorts of creatures and agencies, what is it you want to defend?

– I'm not quite sure what you mean, but justice, of course!

– Justice is just a huge and rather empty word. They do not want to hurt you, those who you are fighting. What are you really afraid of? The quiet and the emptiness?

I did not understand what he meant, and I wanted to end the chat, get up and ride home. Now Peter was beginning to get smart with me!

– Maybe they have offended me? I exclaimed.

– Yes, they may have offended you. Just taste that word, *offended*. You're so good with words. Have they come up too close? It's about time to get them off your end ...

– I just want to be treated like everyone.

–You are a fascinating and interesting chatterbox. You have learned to cope with much of what is bothering you, such as drinking. But how about closeness, presence?

Now I was itching all over, my mouth is a desert and I experienced a desperate need for a beer.

– Now you're probably in desperate need for a beer, am I right?

– Getting drunk was just an excuse, because ...

I couldn't find the proper words anymore. Because what?

– Because of all the other ladies. And how to get rid of them.

Peter must have read my thoughts. I'd better leave, rather suddenly.

– You said, "Finally I drank her up." And how did you excuse yourself to her?

– I didn't. I never did! It must have been a misunderstanding, that lovely lady in love with me? A schmuck like me? No way. I had to make them understand, I had to make them leave, for their own good, all the beautiful ladies ... how did they end up in my bed? Did they not realize that ... Obviously they didn't. So I had to help them out, show them the exit sign.

– In other words: You drank them up?

Clever guy, that Peter. But yes, eventually they all left. Eventually. And I was right, again: I'm no good.

– But what if it was my entire fault, that I staged the whole show, only to be abandoned. For if I wasn't abandoned when it was going so wel l... I could not risk ... it could be getting downright ...

... pleasant ...

– Yes, and what would you risk? Come on now!

– I could risk feeling ... closeness! And then it would all ... I would ... explode into a thousand pieces!

I hit the table hard with my fist, but Peter is not even shrugging.

– Not you. You would not explode, but maybe some of your defenses.

– Maybe all my defenses.

– But that is not so important. You can have good reasons to fight abuse and injustice, but if it becomes a mania, you may cover it out of a fear of going after the important matters, such as ...

– ... my own fear of intimacy. My fear of the hugging hell.

23

... AT THE
END OF THE DAY

I went home. The simplest is the most ingenious, I believe. When you just turn around to face what you're afraid of, and alas: no one is there – you are able to just go on. I am afraid of intimacy; towards myself, towards all others and the world around me. All the other problems I can manage, I know how to handle this drinking and the forgetfulness and the lack of concentration and the boredom and ... But intimacy? And the constant nagging anxiety? So I quit. For five successive years I quit drinking completely.

And suddenly one day, as I was doing ... nothing special, I noticed that the urge was gone. The permanent unease in my belly – the aching, the unease, the nagging uncertainty in my stomach ...
GONE!

Part Three:

NORWEGIAN WOOD: AVOID THE VOID

24

THE TEMPERANCE SEVEN

In the early 1960's, there was a very successful jazz group called *The Temperance Seven*. They had a smash hit with "You're Driving Me Crazy" from 1961 and later with "Pasadena", and a come back ten years later with Petula Clark, doing their version of "Sgt Pepper" in 1971. You'll find them on YouTube. Put them on, while I'm listing up seven myths for you about abusing alcohol – and we can call those marks for *The Temperance Seven*.

I now assume you have read all of this book so far, and that you are exercising your will not to drink for a year. It is of no importance where you are inside of this time frame, but remember: You have to remain a teetotaler for an entire year. You can not take a break, or fall off the wagon: Meaning that you can't allow yourself to get soaked every now and then, only to return to your decision of one entire year's temperance. It *HAS* to be one year. Obviously, there were a number of reasons. Rather, not so obviously, but eventually the obvious will be presenting itself. For now you just have to trust ... yourself.

So, if you break down and fall off that wagon, you have to start climbing back on board all over again. But again: Let's assume you have just gotten sober, and are determined to quit. For a year. No matter how the wind blows. You are rather tranquil, you can manage both reading and keeping your food down and sleep has found you. Now, go to work! If you still have a work to go to, do so and stick to your job. If you for some reason are out of work, take up routines that look like a work: Regularity is of essence. Go to the library, go for some long walks in the neighborhood, visit the churchyard, the railway station, the local pet shop – or whatever fits your geography and your narrative. Everyone has got an individual story, or else it's about time to get started with that story.

Anyway, – routines are what you need. Also for creating some free time afterwards, in which you can ponder about these seven myths about drinking.

Temperance One:

Drinking alcohol is addictive. To be honest, it is not quite that simple. But bear with me. First of all: Both alcohol, heroin, morphine and related drugs are not uppers, they are sleeping remedies – means and agents to induce sleep. Just think about the name "morphine" – the drug is derived from opiates, but the name is derived from Morpheus, the name of the god for dreams from the Greek mythology. So when you are sipping from your bag of wine, you are really in want of sleep. And maybe, on a deeper level, The Big Sleep.

But that aside, we have to specify: *Alcohol* is not addictive, but *drinking* can be. By that I mean *the act of drinking* can be addictive. The substance is not, but the activity might be. That's why you should refrain from replacing drinking with religion, or gambling, or any activity that in fact is compensating for the lack of drinking. One can be as *addicted* to any odd activity, and thus you haven't really evolved away from addiction.

But one can hardly be addicted to alcohol. Think about it: Most people do not have problems with drinking alcohol. Either they almost do not drink, or they have some drinks every now and then, and sometimes a few too many – but they sleep it off, and the last thing they want when they wake up, is another drink. The mere thought will usually nauseate them. Only hard and stubbornly purposeful practice for quite some time, can make you familiar with the concept of relief–ing, of having a hair of the dog that bit you. That is, stomaching a beer or a Bloody Mary as quick as possible after sleeping off the booze, to prevent your system from sobering up. But mind you: This first drink in the morning will almost always be a bungy–shot: It's poison. As sleeping agents usually are.

So: Alcohol is not addictive, the activity of drinking might be. I am here to steer you away from any other captivating activity, so you could have a fair chance to be meeting up with yourself. It might be interesting: Most of your family and colleagues already think you are just that: Interesting.

Tobacco is addictive. In spite of all the hard labour you put down just to familiarize yourself with the substance, it is almost impossible to get totally rid of that vice. My father, a heavy smoker, told me that he dreamt he was smoking, even some twenty years after he had quit. He suffered severely from asthma, so his physician gave him two choices: Either quit smoking, or die. He quit. And lived on, dreaming about smoking.

I was a moderate smoker. But still I miss the cigarette every day after breakfast, and after dinner ... get the picture? Also when it comes to tobacco, which *is* addictive, you can ease the quitting by changing or avoiding the situations when you absolutely needed a fag. For instance when you are having a drink ...

Just to sum up: You don't easily get hooked on either tobacco or alcohol. Those drugs need hard labour to get familiar with, which is a good thing: They are both amongst the most lethal of drugs. One of my friends died of COLD (Chronic Obstructive Lung Disease), half a year after he quit smoking. And how about Richard Burton – he quit drinking alcohol, but his internal organs were so severely damaged that he was beyond salvation. And who wants to operate a kidney on a notorious drunkard? *Once a drunkard, always a ...* more of that later. The substance itself is not easily addictive, but the situations surrounding the indulgence are. That's why both the substances can be categorized as "agents" – for sleep, for dieting/relaxing/alerting... it's only an agent. If so, the serious part of the art of quitting is not to throw your hand, but to change the play. Or the rules of the play.

One word of wisdom: "The town may be changed, but the well cannot be changed." (From *I Ching*, nr. 48, "The Well"). Prophecies and predictions can be addictive as well – and the well might run dry. As it is well known, Adolf Hitler always consulted astrologers before making any decision about the ongoing warfare. The science fiction author Philip K. Dick was also using this dependence on prophecies in his novel *The Man in the High Castle*: The *I Ching* is prominent here; having diffused it as part of their cultural hegemony overlordship of the U.S. Pacific Coast, the

Japanese – and some American – characters consult it, and then *act* per its replies to their queries. Specifically, the *I Ching* replies with Hexagram 61 ([中孚] zhōng fú) Chung Fu, "Inner Truth", describing the *true* state of the world–every character in *The Man in the High Castle* is living a false reality.

And my advice is: You have to change *the town* (meaning turf, bar, gang) anyway, because otherwise you will never find the path to your own Inner Truth. And you have to, in order to get well.

Temperance Two:

And not only is alcohol not addictive, drinking alcohol is not a disease. You are exercising your own free will when you are drinking. To put it bluntly: You have to will yourself to drink. Therefore, no two drunkards are telling similar stories. The drinking pattern is almost as individual as your fingerprint. Just ask around! The variations are plentiful: The reasons for starting to drink, the amount one can stomach, the degree of blank shame and *alcoheimers*, the ability to perform in any faculty. As a writer, my experience is to put down the pen after the first beer. Renowned authors have different experiences with drunk writing. The world famous Nobel Prize winner Knut Hamsun invented a fly swatter under the influence. He found this manual on his bedside, complete with drawings: "Take two pieces of wood, exhibit A and B. Place the fly on Exhibit A, and clap exhibit A and B together. The fly will now be extinct."

Jack London had another MO: "I began to anticipate the completion of my daily thousand words by taking a drink when only five hundred words were written. It was not long until I prefaced the beginning of the thousand words with a drink." Ernest Hemingway had this mantra: "Write drunk; edit sober." Literature is full of authors claiming they write better when drinking, and thereby withholding the myth that alcohol is helping your creativity. And myths are a pregnant part of art. Alcohol is not. Because no one is interested in the fact that almost all our artists are dead sober when they perform. Like everyone else is. And how fun is that to read about?

But as the quotations above illustrate: The stories of drunk writing are different. Hamsun moved into a hotel to write another novel, and started the writing process with drinking whiskey for a fortnight. But not writing a word he could use. London drank all the time, and Hemingway drank and wrote, but edited afterwards. Presumably when he had sobered up.

And this is pretty much the situation with every aspect of the drinking process: Not two stories are similar. Therefore you have to find your own path out of the wood of drunkards, and into a state we could call *Under Milk Wood* – after Dylan Thomas, another drunkard. And poet. My point is that the voices of drunkards may sound hoarse and out of tune, but each end every one is singing her or his own song, no matter how faceless, shameless and nameless they seem, in the wood of drunkards. By underlining the fact that every story is unique, they appear more like all the named characters of *Under Milk Wood*. Before we all appear legless on Boot Hill. Or in *The Spoon Hill Anthology*.

Temperance Three:

A fellow Norwegian scientist, together with two other Norwegians and one American researcher, launched an essay where they claimed that the main cause for alcoholism for 71 percent of the abusers is *hereditary* and therefore *genetic*. That is bull, of course. I know that this is a very popular line of arguing in certain academic circles for the time being, bringing us back to the late fifties and early 60's, when the now infamous professor Burrhus Frederic Skinner put people into his horrible Skinner box and tried to correct people's behavior as were they pigeons. Hence the *behaviorism*, as the name of his theory goes: You can *correct* people's behavior by applying punitive discipline – otherwise known as the stick and the carrot.

Only people are not pigeons. We are not programmed *Norwegian* by our genes to be automatically homing when abroad by some charts imprinted in our cerebrums – most of our behavior we have to learn. If I was born in Afghanistan, my language would have been another, and I most certainly would have been of the Islamic faith. But whether a Sunny or a Shia? Here location and tribe is of essence –because 80percent of the Afghanistan people are Sunnys, and the rest are Shias. But none of this is written in our genes. Being born in Scandinavia, there is a good chance

I would belong to the Protestant church, but in Spain? Some argue that we are born with the need for, or talent for religion, but that is to be debated. What congregation we will attend to, is anyway decided by tribal and trivial factors.

With language, the situation is somewhat similar – and different. Because both religion and language seem to be skills that distinguish people from animals. Man's ability to transform reality into symbols, is species–specific. Other primates may have means of communication, but they lack language. And therefore also lack the ability to develop systems of classification, like religion. Or science. In times when our manufactured cultures are under pressure, language and religion may offer salvation – or suppression. Daniel Defoe's novel *The Life and Strange Surprising Adventures of Robinson Crusoe* from 1719 is a blatant example of this situation. But also a problematic one, if the story is seen from the perspective of Man Friday.

Somewhat more prophetic was William Golding's novel *Lord of the Flies* from 1954. Children surviving a plane crash on a desolated island divide themselves into two groups, eventually fighting each other to the death over the question of belief, and language – symbolized in a pig's head: What does the head mean? Exactly the same existential question as in Samuel Beckett's play *Waiting for Godot* from 1949. Or as the encyclopedia for drunkards have it: "**drinking with Godot** adj. drinking while waiting for friends who may or may not arrive."

But during the summer of 2011, when American psychiatrists were on the verge of launching the *Diagnostic and Statistical Manual of Mental Disorders* (DSM–IV), my Norwegian fellow scientists plus one American, Eivind Ystrom, Ted Reichborn–Kjennerud, Steven H. Aggen, and Kenneth S. Kendler, politely enough presented the results from their research upon male drunkards with the article "Alcohol Dependence in Men: Reliability and Heritability" in the journal *Alcoholism: Clinical and Experimental Research*. There are some nice figures there, too!

But also some hideous claims, namely that our drinking habits as grown ups are dictated by the genes we have inherited, and thus we can proceed claiming that it isn't my fault, I am disposed for drinking. It's in my genes! And though they claim to use strictly academic methods to measure that this heritability applies for 71percent of male abusers, have they actually studied the genes in question? By no means. They have been interviewing male, white identical twins in Virginia. They have been talking to male abusers about their abuse?

On the one hand one could argue that abusers seldom talk truthfully about their abusing habits, but then on the other hand very few of the culprits really turned up, so in fact they were interviewed over the telephone, and then we have no interview, but rather a questionnaire. And that means we have moved from a qualitative state of producing data to a more quantitative one: Counting heads. Which gives us 71 percent abusers from genetic and heretic reasons.

Thus they might design this beautiful definition of the men in question as "**MVVD** n.: *Male Vertical Volume Drinkers; someone, usually male, who consumes an excessive amount of alcohol while standing up.*" (Also from the same encyclopedia as mentioned above). Skol! This whole new–positivistic approach is a reaction to the postmodernism of certain academic disciplines for the last decades, but the paradox of it all is that with the contemporary individualism growing almost to the extreme, leading academic milieus are advocating the idea that the main features of our character is actually predetermined. Our fate lies in our genes.

This line of thinking is old fashioned, and not at all helpful. In the fifties, drunkards could blame their drunkenness on bad genes; before they got *disposed of* for being drunk, they could claim they were skunked because they were *disposed for* being drunk. The consequence of scientific reports as the one quoted above, is that alcoholism should be regarded as an illness: This frees the individual from any will of his own: I am drunk because I am ill, and better still: I have inherited it. So just keep on swallowing.

But I am myself a living proof of another line of arguing: The misuse of any substance is a choice you have made. It is within the range of your free will to end the abuse at any time. It takes some discipline and lots of efforts, but it is doable. You have to will drinking, just as you must will not to drink. You are an individual in your own right, and even God, for those who believe in him, guarantees your free will. According to my own scientific horizon, there exists a more balanced and relativistic interpretation of almost everything. But you have to believe in your own will, and therefore believe that not drinking is doable. Almost everything else is debatable. I don't even believe in The Big Bang. That theory most definitely opens up for a God, and I am skeptic … While new–positivism needs a quick fix.

Or to quote Douglas Adams: "The Ultimate Answer to the Ultimate Question of Life, The Universe, and Everything is *42.*"

Temperance Four:

And if you exercise your free will as suggested in this book, you will be able to change your drinking pattern. After one year of teetotalism, you can enjoy a glass of wine or three totally at your own will, without being an embarrassment to all and everyone. Including you. And there are many agents out there willing to help you. And they may seem unselfish, but might anyway provide an alternative avenue of abuse – or a compensatory misuse.

For instance, religion. In my country, temperance is often paired with religion. If you are an active participant of the parish's daily work, you are not expected to even touch alcohol. This fact has been immensely helpful to many a drunkard. But by joining a religious group you are still under the influence, only the remedy you are using is guaranteeing you a long life and good health. But you will be under constant surveillance, scrutinized forever and a day – because you know what they say: Once an alcoholic, always an alcoholic. And you still are: Sober, but under the influence of another regime. More about this in Temperance five.   The idea is that a drunkard is abusing alcohol in order *to forget*. This is the content of hundreds of jokes: " – Why are you drinking? – To forget. – To forget about what? – *That* I have forgotten". Drinking is an escape, you are a fugitive from yourself. And in that respect the choice of a sleeping remedy is a proper choice. But when your drinking is ruining your family, your work, your life – you have to make a better choice. Or perish.

Being an addict of any medium, means that you develop a series of bad habits. And thereby, all your actions in one way or another is dictated by the pleasing of your bad habit. A gambler is totally under the control of a bookie in one of many versions, a member of a religious group is either constantly collecting money or members or both, a collector is always on the move, chasing new items – the bottom line is: Being an addict, you are always both occupied and pre–occupied. There isn't much room for much else.

But we will not allow any new vice to replace your old friend Al K. Hall. With your own will, you'll be able to examine a wide range of interests that will be conquering for your time. And you will experience that you are going to try out quite a few of these. Some will stay with you for some time, and other activities you will store as fun, but not funny enough. Like golf. (Just an example!) What you would like to avoid, is getting engulfed in an all–time pastime, and thereby meeting two acute needs: The requirement to fill all this newly achieved free time – and the dread for getting accustomed to yourself. And it's scaring the life out of you, no?

One could argue that any activity is preferable to abusing alcohol. Yes, but should you not give yourself the opportunity to take in the wide range of life outside of the bottle, dividing all your fresh, good–looking, nice smelling and delicious phenomenon called Life between a number of interesting activities, and books, and films, and galleries, and friends and lovers and grandchildren and daffodils   and ... The list is infinite. But your time is limited. You dont' want to bag it up in a One and Exclusive Activity. And *Exclusive* means exactly that – you are excluding other options and experiences.

Therefore, by the force of your will to endure one entire and unbroken year of temperance, you will be able to go wherever you want, and even enjoy a glass of wine every now and then. Which is the content of

Temperance Five:

Once a drunkard, always a drunkard. Heard it before? I have tried to find professional evidence of this rather exclusive allegation, but I keep returning to that never ending nature or nurture-debate about heritage and our ability to adjust our behavior, in order to please our environments – our just ourselves. Man is a highly trainable creature.

My assertion is that man is fully capable of altering her or his behavior. What you will have trouble with changing, is your temper. One is more or less dispositional, accustomed to being lazy, hotheaded, lenient, impulsive, phlegmatic ... But with some help, that may be altered too, or you might learn how to control your temper. Or let your impulses run free. And therefore this allegation that once a drunkard, always a drunkard is a brutal one. It is not scientifically sustainable, and that hardcore myth only serves one purpose: You can go on drinking until you reach a natural stop, because that is your nature.

Moreover, this is a self–fulfilling prophecy. Just think about it: There is a strong myth telling you that when a drunkard finally sobers up, it has to be a lifetime commitment. So you are told. And accompanied with tear–jerking stories about that honest and hard–working guy that has been on the wagon for twentyt-hree years, when suddenly this long lost friend turns up from nowhere and lures him into having just this one celebration drink...and suddenly all his achievements get flushed down the toilet.

What actually happens here is that we are inclined to believe all these myths that are engulfing us. Even if they are as real as Santa Claus. The myth says: If you just have one sip of alcohol, you will inevitably continue boozing forever. And well, who can resist nature? Only it is not nature speaking when you order another drink, it is an urban legend. Therefore there is a battle going on inside of you at this crucial moment: What you really want to do, is finish your drink, go home and watch that show on the telly, or polish your mahogany boat from the building kit, turn tatting or whatever. Then there is this voice arguing – ,just one for the road or better: Let's get wasted! And even if you'd rather return to your tatting, you bow your head and surrender. I know, because I've been there many a time and oft. It's like your inner bad cousin persuading your real self – and that's probably exactly what is happening. You are succumbing to our society''s mantra: *Once a drunkard, always a drunkard*. In other words: You are doing your duty to society.

Like the town's drunk Bob Ewell in Harper Lee's *To Kill a Mocking Bird*: He is always around with his bottle concealed in a paper bag. But in the end he reveals that it's all for show: He displays a bottle of coke. He is just paying his toll to the local community, by keeping the place designed for him: The Local Drunk.

By partly opposing this imperative to appear as a drunkard, you might encounter another risk: To develop a pattern of dipsomania. Which means you are drinking on and off: Either all the time, or not at all. At least you get by, in a way, but then again: Half of the time you are out of business. Think of that: Half the year you have no recollection of. One of my fellow inmates at the rehab admitted that he was looking forward to being able to remember the films he was watching.

And: *Dipsomania* is also a compensatory abuse. You have to believe that it is possible to have just a glass of beer or two, just like normal persons do. That was always my dream: Having three pints, and then return home. But usually those refreshments lasted for a week. But first, you need to undergo one year of total temperance.

The funny thing is that the liquor business will embrace my suggestions. After all, civilized drinking is absolutely in their interest, they will welcome considerations about alcohol as the preferred substance in a range of public situations. Rehabs like the Minnesota model and organizations like Alcoholics Anonymous on the other hand...It is rather a paradox that they want to preserve this picture of you as predisposed by your genetics; however, if you are going to administer your own fate and future, they will be out of business, of course. They will claim I'm wrong, but to prove me right, all you have to do is to invest one year of your life. As a bonus, you get to take full command over the remains of your days – with a glass of wine every now and then. And if you encounter difficulties of any kind during this year of temperance - just call me!

But I will take this one step further: Believing the mythos of *Once a drunkard, always a drunkard* can be harmful to your health. And why? Because it invites *Nocebo* in, the harmful brother of *Placebo*. Which is Latin for "I shall please", and refers to a simulated or otherwise medically ineffectual treatment intended to deceive the recipient. Nocebo, though, means quite the opposite: "I shall harm". The term "nocebo response" was coined in 1961 by Walter Kennedy. An example of nocebo effect, or response, would be someone who dies of fright after being bitten by a non-venomous snake.

Which brings me to a book that gave me great pleasure in my rather fresh career as a researcher on indigenous cultures, and more specific: The history, mythology and culture of the Sámis. The book *The Serpent and the Rainbow* was written by Wade Davis, a Canadian ethnobotanist, and issued in 1985. Having finally recovered from the seductive but bogus *Teachings of Don Juan* in the string of books by the student of anthropology Carlos Castaneda, it was quite refreshing to meet a true scientist such as Davis.

From the Sámi culture I had learnt about the Sámi *shaman*, called Noaidi. They were alleged to be in command of certain powers, such as casting spells and bad fortune on people. These were, however, faculties projected on the Sámis by the white cucasian tribes of these circum-polar regions. But the Sámis adapted the whiff of fear and respect that these anticipated qualities earned them among the Norwegian settlers, and went along.

Much the same mechanisms were at work in Wade Davis' Haitian studies. He rendered the case of Clairvius Narcisse, a man that had been a zombie for two years. But as a start, he had heard the rumours of a woman-zombie in the sugar fields of some Central American state that suddenly just lay down her machete and went home. Which suggested that a zombie had some leftovers of free will. So, how does one make a zombie?

The ethnobotanist Wade Davis found that the answer was an interaction of tetrodotoxin, a powerful hallucinogen called Datura. This plant is also called Angel's Trumpet - or Moonflower (!). The active poison can be extracted from pufferfish, porcupinefish, ocean sunfish or mola, and triggerfish - and blocks sodium channels on the neural membrane, produces numbness, slurred speech, and possibly paralysis or even respiratory failure and death in severe cases. As an isolated pharmacological agent, it is not known to produce the trance-like or "mental slave" state typical of zombies in Haitian mythology, or Davis' descriptions, although one might consider the effects of set and setting in combination with the drug.

Of course Davis' findings were opposed , and a scientific debat over his findings took place (Booth, W: (1988), "Voodoo Science" in *Science* 240 (4850): pp 274-277; Hines, T.: (2008), "Zombies and Tetrodotoxin", *Skeptical Inquirer*, Volume 32, Issue 3 (May/June) 1988, pp 60-62; Davis, W.: (1998), "Zombification (Letters)" in *Science:* 1715-1716). It was pointed out that the effects of the agents were too weak to lead to a slave-bound situation, and Davis agreed: It was in combination with the cultural codes such a zombification was possible. When told that you were free to leave, you were free to leave. Hence, the sugar cane cutting woman simply up & went. The curse was broken when people no longer believed in the curse.

But in plain words, a zombification went down like this: The shaman of the Haitian *Vodou* marked out a victim, who would know about the spell about to be adminsitered, and would therefore be cautious with everything consumed, solid or liquid. They knew that there was an agent at large in the zombification process, but suspected some of the local plants to deliver the poison. Hence the caution with digestion. But the poison was extracted from the Japanese Moonfish or some of its relatives in more homely waters, and this poison possessed some inter-dermatological features: it would work even when applied on your skin. So what the *Houngan* or the *Mambo* (female Vodoun priest) did, was to smear the poison on for instance your doorstep right before they know you were bound to step on it. Or your doorknob or anything that suited the mission. And the victim would never know what hit them. And eventually, they died.

But not quite. Because this poison kept the heartbeat to a minimum, and resulted in an almost total respiratory rest. This catatonic situation would last for three days approximately, before the resurrection. Japanese gourmet-chefs know about this side effect of comsuming the belly of the Moonfish, considered as such a delicatesse that it takes seven years of practice to be fully certified as a Moonfish Chef. But just in case, in certain restaurants they keep a couple of beds, should such an incident occur.

After three days, the Houngan gives the victim an antidote-like brew from Datura, you wake up, and you know that now you are a zombie, and that you are under the command of whoever has paid for the services of the Houngan. Therefore, the elements of the culture are really the most effective ingredients of the medicine that creates a zombie. Of course there were other ingredients as well: The *bocor*, Haitian shaman, crushed the skull of a deceased infant, and added it to the poison, freshly killed blue lizards, a large dried toad (*Bafus marinus*) with a dried sea worm wrapped around it (prepared beforehand), *tcha-tcha* (the sub-tropical bush *Albizzia*), and "itching pea" (*pois grater*, a species of Mucuna). But now, when the news is out, this whitchcraft has lost its sting. Just like Antabus. Keep on reading!

You may recollect the episode number fifteen of the second season of the series *X-files*, aired on Fox network on February 3, 1995. It was called "Fresh Bones", and was actually referring to Davis' books on the subject. Therefore, this episode renders a more credible version of the complex of zombification, as does the awful film that Wes Craven made on *The Serpent and the Rainbow*.

Both as a researcher and a former abuser I acknowledged the similarities with certain "treatments" of alcohol abuse. What I have in mind is the vehicle also known as Antabus, in the shape of a Disulfiram implant. A capsule of disulfiram was sewn in under the surface of your skin, and you were told that if you consumed alcohol, this agent would very nearly kill you. Which was bull, of course. There has been much research conducted to actually measure the effect of said agent, and dr. Sanjay Chugh states: "Used alone, without proper motivation and without supportive therapy, disulfiram is not a cure for alcoholism, and it is unlikely that it ill have more than a brief effect on the drinking pattern of the chronic alcoholic." Read more about this phenomenon here: http://doctor.ndtv.com/faq/ndtv/fid/4407/Can_implants_help_a_person_quit_alcohol.html?cp

Or here:

(http://doctor.ndtv.com/faq/ndtv/fid/4407/Can_implants_help_a_person_quit_alcohol.html). But nowadays, this line of therapy is... liquidated.

And therefore, the therapy offered by both the AA and all the different shades of the Minnesota model, is sheer Nocebo: You wouldn't dare touch a drink no matter how many years you have been sober - once a drunkard, you know... And therefore, there was a pretty good chance for you to really go binge drinking forever and a day. But by now, you should know better. I am looking forward to take them on, all those false pushers of Nocebo. Because as you know, *Once a drunkard, change is at hand.*

Temperance Six:

Drinking is an act of will. There is no such thing as accidental drinking – a crate of beer just passed by, so I had to indulge ... Opportunity knocks, so to speak. This is the rather obscure uncle of the more sophisticated, scientifically looking contention that once a drunk ...

And then it's just your old friend Al K. Hall all over again. Or rather Will. You can maintain that the moment you wake up to another day, you can will yourself to avoid using anything stronger than tea and I don't mean *tea* in the Jack Kerouac–ish way, as a nickname for grass, weed, mary jane... but tea. (The sarcastic fact is that Kerouac in his Catholic mind, drank himself to death, in spite of being a Dharma Bum). Even heroin–addicts do have that choice, but of course their abstinence is quite heavy. But they have that choice, every day. And here is a huge and hairy paradox: If asked right to their face, abusers very seldom will claim that the reason for their abuse is their wish to die. But that's exactly what they are doing, they are dying. Abusing alcohol and other drugs is a slow suicide by proxy. A more mundane explanation is the wish to escape from everyday's tiresome claims and routines – they aim for something bigger, something more adventurous, like sailing away in the sunset. But by sunrise they are facing more tedious routines than they possibly can handle: They have to get hold of some serious cash to finance their habits. Therefore, they have to steal something, lifting some old women, pushing drugs to other addicts, even begging on the streets...In other words, you need more hours than a working day contains. Or night, if you are a working girl. Never a day off – all work and no play makes Jack a naughty boy.

The annoying and undeniable fact is there is no other activity on the planet that demands your constant effort so profoundly, as keeping up with your abuse. Every minute is filled with it, every thought also encompasses time, place & amount of said substance, every fiber of your body is preoccupied with the next encounter with your loved one, your wi...sorry, vice.

You get my drift. You have to amount all your will to drag home what's needed to go on feeding your flame. You have to muster all you've got of will, and that's exactly what all this is about: Why not invest your will in ... you've heard all this before? I thought so. Your complete conduct is under the influence of your craving to be wasted all the time, you are a true *social lubricantitus* – Pinocchio–wise. You are always planning meticulously on logistics, the supply situation, potential hideouts for flasks, getting the narratology right, planning your drunk dialing while hopelessly trying not to place the calls, and writing down new ideas for upcoming hangover hookies ...

Very similar to the everyday life of The Honorable Geoffry Firmin, British consul in Malcolm Lowry's novel *Under the Volcano,* taking place in Mexico around 1938 – before the Nazi volcano erupted all over Europe. He managed to get drunk at least twice a day, and like him, you are constantly cheating on the ones you love. Or rather: The ones that love *you,* strangely enough. Because you are being unfaithful, although you are never screwing around. It doesn't matter: You are not available. Either you are out drinking, or you are drunk. I learnt this the hard way when my children let me understand that the moment I downed my first drink, I wasn't there for them anymore. I was not present. In a way I was past present.

Temperance Seven:

Drinking helps you drown the ghosts.

"To be, or not to be", is a well–known quotation by The Bard, William Shakespeare, from *Hamlet*. But more exactly, to be what? "Whether 'tis Nobler opposing them: to die, to sleep no more ... " Hamlet continues. So, this is a question about life or death? The pros and cons of suicide? First we have to establish: *Where* does this Hamlet's soliloquy take place? Not by the grave of poor Ophelia, as most of us believe we remember, no: It succeeds the so called "nunnery scene" in Act 3, Scene 1, where Hamlet discusses the outcome of the dialogue he just had with Ophelia. One could argue that the question of to be or not, rather could be posed as to be *seen* or not to be seen?

Such an interpretation is supported by the sheer location of said soliloquy, namely in the living quarters of the Elsinore Castle. And definitely not by the side of a grave, with a skull in his hand: "That skull had a tongue in it, and could sing once", a tableau that takes place much later, in Act 5, Scene 1. And who did once own that skull? "Alas, poor Yorick!" How could Hamlet be so sure? "I knew him, a fellow of infinite jest". We know that poor Hamlet had recently lost his father, while his mother was busy banging his uncle, and Hamlet is blaming his father who "hath borne me on his back a thousand times; and now, how abhorred in my imagination it is!" Because, as we know, his father died from absorbing liquids of a rather malicious kind, and therefore is to be blamed.

You might object that this was a rather far–fetched interpretation. But the whole set–up is not that far–fetched: *Hamlet* is a play about the need to be seen as who you are. So, as I have already mentioned, the line really ought to read like this: "To be seen, or not to be seen, that is the question." And in our effort to be seen, there is no point in chasing ghosts. Or rather being chased by ghosts, as Hamlet is. His dead father surfaces as a ghost, demanding of his son to revenge his death. But we have to deny such claims, sweeping out all the skeletons.

To put it plainly: You are drinking to drown the chattering skeletons. But as Hamlet experienced: They won't lie down. You have to confront them. The quest is to put an end to the life–threatening situation you are in. For Hamlet it was blood revenge, for you it is abusing alcohol. Different diagnosis, same therapy: You have to quit. But reasonable persons need reasons: Which brought me back in the USSR. That journey helped me deconstruct some rattling skeletons, and paved my road to temperance. There is a dialectical, mutual connection with your past and the immediate contemporary, and an eternal simultaneous movement between those two entities. And then the eternal question is revealed: What comes first, the chicken or the egg? I can't answer that, but here comes the eggs!

25

AVOID THE VOID –
INTRO TO THE MANUAL

Actually, it's all about the old carrot and the stick: Stick, stick, stick ... stick to the water wagon for an entire year, with no glitches whatsoever, and then you can have all the carrot you may desire for the rest of your life.

And why would that work? A debate about the physical and psychological reasons why this actually works so well, – will conclude this book. But now, before we reach to practical advices for dealing with The Void, here are some preliminary exercises: You have to bury the shame, you have to move to another well, and you have to make arrangements with your spouse. If you have any.

SHAME, is the key word here. Our aim is not to become shameless, but to evolve into a state of shame–less–ness: We have to stop running, look behind us, meet the emptiness...and that's why I suddenly remembered Soviet: In order to move on, I headed right back in the USSR. We can only proceed, after having noticed that there are no logical reasons for our shame. Quite the opposite of Marcel Proust's *In Search of Lost Time*; earlier translated as *Remembrance of Things Past*: He never quite got out of bed, where he was busy eating his Madeleine cakes, pondering a verse from the Bible: "Consider the lilies of the field, how they grow: they neither toil nor spin" (Mathew 6:28). But we need to toil and spin, and as freshly sobered up, we absolutely need to constantly consider the lilies. But not only regarding them in the very field, we need to constantly care for them! We have to keep busy, busy, busy! So in our personal search for the lost time, first we have to reconstruct our remembrance of things past. And as time goes by, important clues will click into place in your memory, caring for the lilies of your field grows automatic, until you no longer have to remind yourself about anything concerning drinking: You would be surprised how fast one year elapses.

This reconstruction of highlights from your past is the overall aim for your resurrection – your strive to get acquainted with your sober self. But you can pretty much leave this work to certain elements of your brain: Your excellent hard disk will take care of this process when you are busy doing other things. Like taking care of shame. Our parents, relatives, family, our great expectations, the lot inflict our constant feeling of shame upon us. So we want to sleep it off, and we're helping the nature by consuming more than enough alcohol, and the effects you know too well. In short: We have to face the shame.

I have to underline that by *shameless* I understand a person appearing promiscuous, by showing off. By *shame–less–ness* I mean conducting your usual business with a flair of naturalness, a matter of factly sauntering through the rest of your life. But of course, all this naturalness doesn't come naturally – we have to work on it. And when you have stayed sober for at least a week, and there are only fifty–one more sober weeks ahead of you – here comes The Void. Not at once, not before you have struggled and conquered your inner search for shame. It's all your fault, only you are the one to blame, for everything.

But there's always an explanation to that feeling of shame. In my case, it was my parents. They were both pestered with illness – all my fault, of course. So I felt so shameful that I had to go to extremes to even get their attention: I went to the Soviet Union, to take on Brezhnev, no less! That got their attention. I had my one and only profound talk with my father in prison. Our attempts to conceal our conversation with coded talk all the more highlighted it.

I staged all this brouhaha, and all I revealed was my own shame. You have to consider whether you want to contact professional help in dealing with what you might recognize as *shame*. A therapist might help you, or talks with an old friend, like the talks I have reported from in this book. Talking to the wall will not do the trick, but family might. If you do have a spouse, you have to have rather serious talks with said partner anyhow. We will come to that in a minute.

But spare them for your shame – it might diminish their opinion of you, and you don't need that. If you belong to a church, conversations with the vicar should be considered. And this piece of advice is coming from a man of little faith! But they are trained to take on rather grave dialogues. If you have a Best Friend you could trust, or a trusted colleague ... there must be someone! If not, visit the nearest Alcoholics Anonymous and make a public confession, it helps! I have tried it myself. You could attend to a meeting or two, you could eventually meet someone there who you could have some conversations. It's worth a try.

Before you find someone to confide in, you might start this simple self–analysis by establishing: When did I really start drinking? That question was quite a challenge, and if you recollect, I ended up in the home of the parents of my fiancé, alone with *Sgt. Pepper* – and some bottles of red wine. But my history of abuse was not one of instantly addiction, it seldom is. But the will was there! The will to drink, I mean, and little by little this will is constantly consuming you, until you are drunk. Spoken literally. And soon everything is drunk – your family, your job, your home, your future...the list does not end until you do.

But you have still got your friends! That depends. If you are in a relationship, you have met some new "friends" in addition to your mutual friends. These new "friends" we usually refer to as bad friends – you wouldn't invite them home. You talk football with them – never shop, or books – not to mention politics! The only talk you share with them, is small talk. Very small talk. So when you decide to embark on this one–year's journey, you immediately discover this lack of real conversation. But they will not enjoy your company for long. And the reason is simple: Try to spend some time with them at the pub or bar or wherever you meet for a beer, and experience that they soon will shun you if you are just enjoying a soft drink. Not because they are biased, but rather that they do not like to be spied on.

Most of us are more relaxed about enjoying a drink when we are together with others enjoying a drink as well. Just try ordering a soft drink or water or a non–alcohol beer in a bar, or in a setting that calls for frequently toasting each other, like anniversaries and social events where the guests really are expecting a free drinking ... and then refrain from a drink. See their awkward smiles! Watch how they demand an explanation, listen to their offers to pay your taxi home, to arrange for you to be picked up by their personal chauffeur, to let you have the guest room, to sleep with the wife of the host...Anything at all to make you have a drink as well. Why? Because they are deeply concerned with your comfort? Not at all – they want to have their drink in peace; they do not need sober witnesses.

A drinking situation is one where the strict rules of socializing are somewhat softened. Or – there is another set of rules applying for such incidents. And staying sober is a brutal and impolite violation of these rules. So either you have to leave ... or drink. Blaming it on the car is accepted, but if it happens once more, you don't get invited. Unless you are filthy rich, of course. In that case, you are such an eccentric. And everybody loves a millionaire!

And you will find it awkward to stay on with your fellows after they have started on their third beer for the evening. It is not that they have taken leave of their senses, far from it...Only it is becoming rather boring. They have these pointless discussions, they are repeating the same arguments you have heard a million times before, they might as well show a poster: *Argument No. 5* – and you realize you are in the middle of a never ending loop. You can't take more of it, you can't drink, and it would be rather impolite of you to leave.

So what do you do? You have to change the well. Although *I Ching* claims: "You can change the city, but you cannot change the well", you can counter with good old Heraclitus from Ephesos. You remember him, the *panta rei* guy? "Πάντα ῥεῖ"? You know – "everything flows" – the chief mantra for us intellectual alcoholics. He sticks to the wet elements, here goes another of his doctrines: "No man ever steps in the same river twice". But that's exactly what an alcoholic does – all the time! The question is: Do we ever get *out* of that river? By no means. And here is another piece of wisdom, but this one is homespun: Man is the only creature that is able to reflect upon himself.

If we keep neglecting the lifebuoy someone constantly are throwing at us, until they give up and go home, we will drown. If we ban the beer, we will be banned – if you refuse the beer, you will be refused. Or drowned. There is only one solution: Up and go! You have to change the well. You won't miss them, and you won't be missed. What you will miss is Life, as you know it. No less. But in order to *have* a life for some time, you have to let go. Or rather: You have to go.

If you live in Endora or Reedsburg, you really have to move. In New York or another big city, you just have to find another neighborhood, or another gang to hang with, perhaps just around the corner. In my hometown everybody knew me, or knew *of* me, so I moved to the capital. I dived before I drowned, and surfaced with a new life. But first, I nearly lost my job, and I nearly lost my life. Then I met my wife – she didn't bother my drinking, she didn't try to save me, she respected me for who I was, and for the first time of my life I felt I was seen. She saw me.

And gradually I tried to control my drinking, mainly in order to please her. But her response was that I only must cut down on my consumption, if I really wanted to for my *own* sake. And gradually this statement surfaced again, delivered by two different professionals at two different stages of my life: My psychologist from back when I experienced a couple of epilepsy–like attacks: "Quit drinking for a year, and then you can drink whatever you like for the rest of your life". Of course I didn't believe him, I just planned my drinking better. And years later, my physicist: "Why don't you just quit? It's really a piece of cake".

Ignorants! But eventually, I proved them right. Or I was willing to give them some credit: They might be right. So I quit. And all the above happened, and is bound to happen with you as well. But my wife did not quit, and I resumed my work, and eventually I delivered this assertion I mentioned and became a doctor. I even received a golden ring, to prove my doctorhood! As my old friend from the birth of rock'n roll, Little Richard, exclaimed: "Good Golly Miss Molly!"

But beware of the bride. I have mentioned this before – corking the bottle does have a string of consequences. The most important one is the reaction from your spouse, if you have one. There is a discrepancy between parole and practice in most walks of life. One thing is what the spouse claim – quite another is their reaction if you are getting serious and do what they claim: Stop drinking. You will be transformed. You will change into a totally different person all together – you will become responsible, reliable and predictable, and the paradox is that you therefore have regained control over your own life. Your spouse is no longer in charge. Therefore you are a threat – you might leave them, for example! And maybe that's exactly what you ought to do, in order to take care of yourself: Just leave.

Charles Bukowski said: "Drinking is an emotional thing. It joggles you out of the standardism of everyday life, out of everything being the same. It yanks you out of your body and your mind and throws you against the wall. I have the feeling that drinking is a form of suicide where you're allowed to return to life and begin all over the next day. It's like killing yourself, and then you're reborn. I guess I've lived about ten or fifteen thousand lives now." Exactly. But every drunk has got to stop once in a while – because your body goes on strike. This happens at least twice a year. You simply can't stomach anything, and you have to sober up. Therefore every drunkard has experienced detoxification and abstinence. You stay sober for five days, that's the amount of time needed to restart your feeding and sleeping process. But professional drinkers leave their status as sober as soon as they can eat and sleep – now they are fit for the next rounds.

A famous Norwegian author, Jens Bjorneboe, – a poet, novelist, playwright and a major participant in the contemporary public debate and discourse, once published a poem that ran across an entire page of a major Norwegian newspaper, – it was titled "Goodbye Brother Alcohol". However, he didn't quite manage to quit, he just redefined *alcohol* to be *liquor* and left out beer and wine and some years later he committed suicide. But we could learn something from the title: Alcohol substitutes family. Drinking is all immersive, and should therefore be met with respect. To quit drinking for a year is not going to be a tea party. But quitting is only half of my scheme. The other half is to be able to resume drinking alcohol in a civilized manner after a period as a teetotaler for at least fifty-two successive weeks. One year, but just like this: fifty-two *successive* weeks. And here are some suggestions on how you can divert yourself during this period, in order to keep you away from Booze & Bottle, Inc.:

Here is My Manual:

After the first five days of your soberness have expired, you have restituted your habit of reading, sleeping, and eating solid food. Whether you have a work to attend to or not, you now will experience the full blast of The Void: When you return home after work, after shopping, after a walk or whatever, meaninglessness is confronting you in a head–on collision. Actually you are ready for a drink. Now recollect all those similar episodes when you were ready for a drink that you really did not want – but come on! I'ts Friday night, you have the week end off, there's a show on the telly and the boys are waiting for you... but you'd rather not. In fact, you have to persuade yourself, you have to remind yourself how you have earned this drink ... and you really have to will yourself to swallow that drink.

Cherish that memory, glue yourself to the telly for the entire evening, and I can promise you a memorable awakening the day after: *You won!* You really did! You defeated yourself, the only person who really is a match for you! And never have you felt such a satisfaction as you do now, you are entitled to ... then comes the question of compensatory use. You can't treat yourself with heaps of chocolate, or burgers, or whatever tastes you cherish. You should not replace one line of consumption with anything edible or drinkable. But you could consider films, or theatre, or musicals/operas or any other shows... or newspapers! I spent a whole two and a half week consuming newspapers. I followed the presentation of the same feature in a number of papers, just to spot the angling and the development of the case. All the while I was totally absorbed by music.

And this is how that came around: I was fiddling with my computer, and came across those pages where I could download all sorts of music. You have to bear in mind that those were the days when everything on the Internet was for free – everybody could upload almost anything. I remembered from my early youth, when we were impatiently waiting in the record stores for the latest Elvis. Especially when he returned from the services – we were waiting for weeks on end in March 1960 for "Stuck on You." Now I had to wait for minutes to download the entire album *Elvis is Back!*

For me it was like stumbling over a treasure. I listened for days and nights – downloaded a lot, both golden oldies and pure classic music: As a boy I attended the esteemed boy's choir of the only cathedral of

Norway, in fact the Nidaros Cathedral was my second home – I was more or less abandoned at home. Also more recent popular music, like Justin Timberlake and Nelly Furtado singing "Give It to Me." Something in the sound from what – violins? Or a steel guitar filled with massive sorrow? I don't know. It got to me. It enhanced my permanent feeling of loneliness, and bear in mind that I was happily married. Still am, by the way. I could sit for hours listening to that single, and gradually it evolved into Nelly Furtado's "Say It Right", and she opened up for Radio Tarifa. – For periods of that year, I spent some time in the regions of southern Spain bordering on Portugal – and if you follow my drift you already can see where this takes you: I was stuck on music. As I mentioned, I spent hours roaming the Internet for music I didn't know I enjoyed listening to, and downloaded the lot. Then all this stuff needed to be catalogued, and some chosen items were copied to CDs. And all this technology was new to me, so I had to learn it all, get hold of blank CDs and racks to stack 'em in, and labels to print and Hey! I needed a printer, I had to look for decent fonts for printing the titles, and programs that allowed me to catch, present and print pictures for labels and covers and you know... time went by.

Just to give you some examples: I grew up with The Beatles. "Please Please Me" happened on March 22, 1963, when I was on the verge of the transition from middle school to high school. In addition, the release of the album *Sgt. Peppers Lonely Hearts Club Band* in June 1967 was remarkable in my personal genesis as a drunkard: I have already mentioned the euphoria I felt in the home of the parents of my fiancé's, being alone with the sergeant and his band plus some bottles of claret. In many ways my debut as an abuser of alcohol.

So naturally: I sampled a lot of their hits, got hold of *Help!* and other films staging The Beatles – the most remarkable being *A Hard Day's Night* from 1964. The film was made in the style of a mockumentary, describing a couple of days in the lives of the group. It was directed by Richard Lester, who gave us a string of semi–absurd experiences like *The Knack ... and How to Get It* from 1965, and *Help!* later that year, *The Bed–Sitting Room* from 1969 – then came *Three Musketeer*-films and two *Superman* films– and by that time Lester had lost *The Knack*.

And after having re–experienced both my favorite music and films from the 60's, I rediscovered John Lennon *In His Own Write* from 1964, followed by *A Spaniard in the Works* the year after. Penguin issued them both in one paperback as *The Penguin John Lennon* in 1966, with John posing in a quasi–Superman suit on the cover. And as you can see – sampling some favorite hits from the 60's opens up an entire universe of Beatlemania and memorabilia. But there are other favorites – as Miles Davis. Gradually he had been influenced by electric sounds that he brought into his band from 1967. He might perform with his back towards the audience, but he was fronting the electronic development with eagerness. His double album *Bitches Brew* was released on August 19, 1969, the day after Jimi Hendrix's sunrise set concluded the now–legendary Woodstock Music and Art Fair. Miles Davis appeared at the Molde Jazz Festival in Norway in 1984. And 1985.

On *Bitches Brew*, he was featuring, amongst others, Chick Corea. Unfortunately, I did not attend to the Miles Davis–gigs in Molde, but I experienced Chick Corea live at the same scene in 1972. That same year he released his first *Return to Forever*–album, and some of the compositions were performed in that concert. I was there, and I was enjoying a reefer that was sent my way. Although I purchased the album later on, playing it never gives me the same chill that I got in Molde. Maybe if I put on some clogs, and invite a crowd of 3000 of my nearest friends ... to restitute that night in Molde. Or maybe it was something I smoked?

The summer of '72 I lived in the vicinity of Molde. I had been teaching at a school in the village where my mother grew up, and my friend from San José visited me. He brought some acid, so we didn't have to ski. It was the strangest of experiences, but I decided never to try it again. The possibilities were too scary, even for me, the high sensation seeker. Instead, we hiked through some of the most picturesque mountain massives of Norway. We actually hitched and hiked our way from the city of Kristiansund to Trondheim, some 250 kilometers in all. Hitchhiking with some cars, a couple of ferries and then hiking through the mountains, quoting Nietzsche. Or was it Alfred E. Neuman? You didn't fancy that one – but...what, me worry?

But before that, I met The Doors. I visited Mike, my Californian ski–compadre, in San José in 1965, as a sailor on a freighter. He took me to the beach of Santa Monica, and there I met Jim Morrison and John Densmore. Just walking along the beach. Mike went bananas, but I didn't even notice them. He pointed out Morrison to me, and you never forget the looks of him. Not only extremely good–looking, but magnetic in some mysterious way. And by this time, August 1965, they were just a rumor in campuses nationwide. They appeared in some nightclubs, like London Fog and Whisky a Go–Go. But only a year later, in August 1966, the band did have their break through, with their single *Break On Through (To the Other side)*. But I already had a bootleg that Mike sent me. And I had actually met him! If I only knew … But besides his music and lyrics, we also sheared another mutual interest, Jim and I: Whisky. Probably cost him his life, but I'm still around …

I'm still around, thanks to all this music, the films they led me to and also all these books, but most important is my will to administer all these impulses. I know that Jim Morrison enjoyed all the illegal substances that came his way, as did the Beatles – with one exception: Heroin. That substance is a killer. And it is also highly addictive. As is the music by the Beatles, but it doesn't kill you. Alcohol does, but it is debatable if that substance is addictive or not, but nobody opposes to putting tobacco on that list of addictive substances. And it kills, too. In different ways – cancer or COLD.

But these freewheeling associations are not only including rock and pop music. I mean, The Doors stole their name from a novel by Aldous Huxley: *The Doors of Perception* from 1954, where he rendered his impressions from taking mescaline – he had much the same experiences as visualized in the biopic *The Doors* by Oliver Stone in 1991. But the title was also stolen by Huxley, namely from the poem *The Marriage of Heaven and Hell* by William Blake, from 1790. The year after, Wolfgang Amadeus Mozart died in Vienna, one of music's absolute geniuses. He was just thirty-five years old, and speculations had it that he probably was poisoned. This was the narrative in another biopic, by Milos Foreman this time: *Amadeus* from 1984, where fellow composer Antonio Salieri confesses to the murder of Mozart thirty-two years ago.

But those ports could open up on other gates, for instance *The Grate Gates of Kiev* by the Russian composer Modest Petrovitsch Mussorgsky (Моде́ст Петро́вич Му́соргский 1839–1881), probably renowned for his *Night on Bald Mountain*, as performed in Disney's very modern and experimental film *Fantasia* from 1940 (!), where the musical score was conducted by Leopold Stokowski. *The Great Gates of Kiev* leads us to the cycle of piano pieces called *Pictures at an Exhibition* from 1874. Maurice Ravel orchestrated them in 1922. You know, the guy with *Bolero*? A bit less modest that version than Modest Mussorgsky's original score; and even bordering on bold, was Emerson, Lake and Palmer's version from 1972. We bought a copy in Kristiansund that very year when my friend the skier from California returned my visit. And all this because I met Jim Morrison on a beach in California in 1965? I could go on endlessly with these associations – and my advice is: ***Follow the flow***. And still I haven't reached Leningrad.

All these flashbacks on music and books and other substances are tools I use in my effort to demonstrate what happens to you when you refrain from alcohol for weeks and months on end: You can follow your associations. They don't get abrupt by the next drink, or the planning of the next drink, or the regrets over that last drink or the disastrous situation when you discover that you are out of alcohol, or wife and children, or work, or housing... or all the above mentioned.

In this transition that I suggest, your associations are fully operative, and they can take you places! So hang on there, you are going places, just one single year of teetotalism – and I can promise you: Then you will have your life back. And you will be going places. *There's a Fog upon LA* so I sampled from the band Chicago from the city of Chicago, Illinois, who brought me back to a *Saturday in the Park*, also in the summer of '72. On the beach of Las Palmas I listened to Queens *Radio Gaga*, but suddenly I got the wind of Radio Tarifa in the Jerez region of Spain, where I met Lady Gaga. Well, not in person, but what, me worry?

And thus I was on my way to The Great Barrier Reef.

26

FACE THE VOID –
THE MANUAL CONTINUED

And as you have already understood: That is the superior and overall idea: Making time disappear, or more brutally: Killing time. I became a mass destructor of idle time. And why? Because I needed desperately to develop measures of masking The Void: When you sober up, all those things you haven't been doing for some time, is savagely demanding your undivided attention. Therefore you are eating all the time, trying to flush down a couple of stacks with apple pie and ice cream and brownies and cherry coke accompanied by seventeen different tastes of coffee – all at the same time. While reading three papers and novels as you are watching TV – and sex! You can't get enough, your schedule is full but still there is this constant tapping in your head, as if someone is begging for your attention.

And it is. Your thoughts are tapping at the rostrum of your mind, demanding the floor. But you won't allow them. They are the reason you started to drink in the first place, remember. All those tedious thoughts, mostly about guilt and shame and lack of an honorable life ... sooner or later you have to face them, you need to get to know your inner narcissist. Only then you can achieve the necessary damage control. But not right now. So you roam around, listening to all that music wrapping up your threatening thoughts.

In those days I rediscovered my bike and the pleasures of cycling around, following known but unfamiliar roads and paths all over the countryside. Or mostly: Inside my city and its suburbs. I filled my flask with some tasty energy drink, put some fruits in my saddlebags, some books and a blanket and rode on into the sunset. And always with music in my ears. I had this fabulous new machine in my pocket, connected a headset to it with a device that let me switch between radio and my own canned music – I could even use it as a telephone! And after receiving a call, the music automatically came back on, while I was riding along on my bike.

Sheer happiness! Plus I got some desperately needed exercise for my body. Which is of paramount importance for your persistent well-being. And you need to get in shape rather quickly. Might I suggest that you start with some interval training? By simple means, and by stealing as little as possible from you precious time (I was being sarcastic), you can climb from no constitution at all to a rather decent fitness in a week or two: Find a stretch, preferably on a dirt road, for example between lamp posts. Run as hard and fast as you can for approximately fifty meters, or from one lamp post to the next, then jog as slow as you can for the next fifty, and then full throttle for the next fifty ... you get the picture? Repeat this sequence ten times (five full speed plus five times slow speed), and keep up this practice for a week or two. After that, you need to jog or walk briskly for at least half an hour per day for the rest of your year of temperance.

After a couple of weeks you should be able to climb ten floors without gasping. And from now on you are on your own. Practice–wise, that is. I would suggest jogging for half an hour daily five days a week – or a brisk walk, as I mentioned. *Exercise is Medicine* is an American program for a weekly schedule of moderate exercise that would reduce your risks for a premature death caused by cardial problems by 40%. (Here: http://exerciseismedicine.org/documents/PublicActionGuide_LR.pdf). From the recommendations: "150 minutes a week of moderate intensity, or 75 minutes a week of vigorous-intensity aerobic physical activity. Muscle-strengthening activities that involve all major muscle groups performed on 2 or more days a week." This applies for Adults 18-65, with "No Chronic Conditions" (ibid.). You could keep up with that, easily.

And also music–wise you'll notice that your need for staying connected all the time, is fading as time goes by. But by these simple steps you are feeding the needs of both body and mind, as the Beatles so neatly put it: "Keeps my mind from wandering". But that was why you started to drink in the first place, wasn't it? To escape your mind's wandering and pondering? Another paradox for you there, but for the time being The Void is lurking in this massive and impenetrable jungle that is your re–opened brain.

And your overall feelings in these challenging times of temperance are perhaps restlessness and lack of concentration. Therefore you might appear as somewhat hyper–active – and therefore I asked for professional help, mostly for sorting out all these new emotions and impulses and unknown abilities, and I needed some distance in order to concentrate on my work. But by that time I was already sober – and had been for more than a year. Only in hindsight did I notice this, but now I am shearing this piece of experience with you: Step by step you will recognize yourself. And that is literally what you are working on: – **re–** is Latin for *over again*, **cog–** is from the Latin word "cognitio" for *knowledge, notice, perception*, and the – **nize**–thing is signaling the verb function of the word. So: **recognize** means *getting to know yourself – anew*. Simple? But then again I'm a doctor.

But I am anticipating your development. As you already have gathered, the crucial thing is to stall The Void from engulfing your mind totally. It is possible "With a little help from your friends", or totally on your own: It's all "Within you and Without you" – and in such cryptically Beatlical terms I am speaking about your will, of course. But you already understood that much. To clear your mind, you could put on *Good Will Hunting* – the breakthrough film for actor Matt Damon.

And I am not joking. First of all, that film is all about recognizing your own potentials. And secondly, watching films is a reasonable way of killing time. You know, fifty-one more weeks, three hundred and sixty days, 8640 hours minus 2520 hours for sleeping, which makes 6120 hours for watching films. Approximately 3060 films. But seriously, you need to find the medias that suit you. I more or less stumbled over music, which developed into some sort of a hobby: Collecting, looking for samples, sampling, cataloguing and storing on different platforms, which brought about some fresh orientation in the fields of electronics. Watching film was another preferred pastime. And this activity also lead to a range of other activities, and my surroundings kept filling up with dead bodies of time... But in the dead of night I was asleep.

And time goes by.

The key word here is that any activity you might choose, will be generating more activity. I mentioned a hit by Nelly Furtado, and her Spanish last name lead me to Radio Tarifa, the Spanish group with a mixed and jazzy sound of flamenco, rock, Arab music; in short – a Mediterranean sound. And although the group stems from Madrid, the name is adopted from a small *ciudad* at the very tip of the Iberian Peninsula. If you are driving from say Malaga, you have to pass Algeciras, the port of the ferries for Africa, and Gibraltar, this encapsulated English town from the mid– fifties. At the pubs here, you will find probably the best steak and kidney pie in England! Therefore, they keep on staying here, the English; to the rage & fury of the surrounding Spain. The whole thing is rather peculiar.

But there you go! The whole idea is to follow the associations popping up. So this geography lesson hopefully gives you an idea of where I'm going: On the pursue of successful time killing, I am placing your attention on the spot of Europe with the shortest distance from Africa. From here you can take ferries to Tunisia, Algeria, Morocco ... A visit to Tanger in Morocco is only an hour away. But of course, for a North American Mexico is in the vicinity, and there you'll find Spanish talking people – but also Ibogaine clinics ... But more of that later.

But our *imagination* of Africa can happen instantly. And equipped with your freshly achieved soberness and the will to stay sober for an entire successive year, you will pursue down a plentitude of paths that are now open for you to investigate. Most of them will prove to be of little interest, but quite a few seem intriguing. And since you are by no means of a bipolar state of mind, you will spend as much time as you feel like, on this trail to Southern Spain or Mexico and beyond. You might pick up some Spanish (I did!), you might come across this peculiar local language of Gibraltar, namely *Spanglish* – a mixture of English and Spanish that constitutes a certain verbal merge of two different languages, with a function somewhat similar to *cockney*: The origin is the need for ordinary people to protect themselves linguistically from the ruling classes – Spanish or English nobility and gentry. But nowadays, both linguistic varieties have their own dictionaries.

Or you could learn something about Flamenco, gypsies and *The Moor's Last Sigh*. As you probably know, the Arabs colonized parts of Spain for centuries, until Boabdil, the last Moorish king of Grenada left the palace of Alhambra in 1492, much to the passionate protests from his mother. You'll find this story inspiringly rendered by Salman Rushdie in his novel with that title. This explains why there are some many words and names of Arab origin in the Spanish language. You could pursue that Arab track and learn about the difference between Moors and Arabs.

Moor stems from Greek, and means "black." But were the Moors really black? Another interpretation – and this I have from a Moorish professor of language I met in Tanger – is that the Greek meant that the indigenous people they met in Morocco talked a language that sounded like *berber*, an onomatopoetic meaningless babble. And suddenly you've got another people – the Berbers! And if you dig deeper in these matters, you will learn that ancient kings of Northern Africa for several centuries captured as many as a million European slaves, from as far as Iceland! I recommend history professor Robert Davies of Ohio State University and his book *Christian Slaves, Muslim Masters: White Slavery in the Mediterranean, the Barbary Coast and Italy, 1500–1800*. (Informations here: http://www.palgrave–usa.com/catalog/product.aspx?isbn=0333719662).

And maybe thus the indigenous peoples in Northern Africa not necessarily appear as – again: Black. And the typical Spanish culture is nothing but a mixture of all these Mediterranean cultures: The singing that accompanies the Flamenco is partly of African origin, as is the Portuguese Fado, and partly an offspring of the Gypsy culture. But wait a minute ... *gypsy*? From the name of Egypt, and the name indicates that the British colonizers wrongly assumed that the gypsies really came from Egypt. But both the dance and the guitar of the Flamenco the Spaniards have adapted from the Gypsy culture, that were run out of Spain to Portugal in the roaring 1490's, and later form Portugal as well. Together with the Sephardic Jews, by the way ... And you might end this flight of the Condors with a paperback by the late John Lennon, *A*

Spaniard in His Own Write, and he was shot in New York and suddenly you are home again.

This goes on and on, and by now I am totally off the rocker. Which was the idea, of course. My point is that in order to cope with The Void, you better pick up some activities that are amusing and fun to do. In real life, however, you are hardly picking up any *new* activities, it's rather a matter of *re*–cognition, as mentioned previously – you are *re*–learning things you knew from before. And besides, all learning is a change of experience, as I believe the famous pedagogue Jean Piaget claimed. I do not have to agree totally, but we are borne almost without any experiences at all. And once you have parked the bottle and do raise your head above the usual abyss of lies and covert drinking and hullabaloo that you believe nobody notices, you recognize life as it once was.

But alas, it is not that easy. Why should anyone believe you? You are really out on a limb here, and you are totally on your own. You better assume that, or else ... A passage from one of Carl Hiaasen's books comes to my mind; I don't recall which one, for I have read them all. These weird environments of villains and gangsters and a few honest people of Florida seems to me somewhat ... familiar – here people appear in a weird but recognizable way. One of the culprits of one of these hilarious novels have a scam going for himself – he pretends he's so incapacitated that he can only move around in a wheelchair. He therefore collects the dole and other unlawful benefits designed for *minusvalidos*, and lives off state and municipal welfare. Until one day that he really needs to get around; he rises from the chair, aiming for a few steps away from danger, but immediately tips over: He has been sitting too long in this bogus wheelchair, and has totally lost his mobility. He has lost the knack.

But you haven't. You only need some practice. And therefore, you need your body to be operating at the top of its capacity. So please go back and repeat those few lines I wrote on your daily fifteen–twenty minutes of training intervals: five lengths fifty (or hundred) meters full throttle, fifty meters jogging, then fifty meters full speed, and repeat this torture ten times. You can afford an hour five days a week (man needs to rest!) – thirty minutes practice, half an hour for preparations and shower and combing your hair; the works.

Avoid The Void – that is the question. Not *To be, or not to be.* That's next in line, though. But first you have to survive. For the time being you are busy admitting that for those past years, you have loved your bottle over everything. Your mother, your spouse, your children ... and even if you haven't been cheating or sleeping around, your spouse is right when she/he accuses you of being unfaithful. Because your bottle is your belief, and *Thou shalt not ...*

A description a little less harsh: Your life has been permanently set on "hold." But to avoid any "fast forward" – movements, which almost certainly will lead to a relapse, you have to establish a certain fixed concentration on your inner turmoil. And my advice is to stick to one or a few of your preferred activities, and immerse into those waters for a while. This is to avoid conquering chaos with more chaos, and slowly filling The Void with meaningfulness, instead of trying to avoid it. In plain words: Instead of avoiding The Void, turn around slowly and face it with one or a couple of your favorite activities.

I have studied indigenous cultures for a lifetime, and especially the Sami culture. I wrote my doctoral dissertation on the works of a Sámi author and sculptor, and in their language lies an important kernel of philosophy: In most Latin–based European languages the most important sentence goes like this: "I have money". Translated to the Sami language, this sentence reads: "Mii læt ruðat" – "money is with me". Which means that Sámi is a *be*–language, while ours is a *have*–language. Which means a lot when it comes to the rather existential question about how we perceive Life. We must admit, earning money and/or owning things is the driver of the main Western cultures. While the Sami originally have a tribal way of life, they were semi–nomads who moved among three–four dwellings throughout the year. They did not entertain flocks of reindeers until around 250 years ago, and they did never "own" the deers – they just lived together with them. Therefore the Sámi have very few words for the ownership phenomenon, and that's why this is a culture of *do*–ers more than *have*–ers, if you read me right.

Let's not lose ourselves in philosophical or philological aspects, but rather take this linguistic difference as a hint: Let your mind flow. Let one or a couple of activities come to you to be with you for a while, rather than invade, or being invaded by, one hobby: Collecting art belongs to me! It's far better to start following a path that seems the most inviting. Become an existentialist for a period – or try out the *I Ching*: Throw your coins, make out the hexagram they are pointing to, and scrutinize the interpretation. Or take up genealogy, which you have been planning for some time. As a professional reader, I decided to read all the Nobel Prize laureates in literature – do you have any idea how many of them are from United States? Ten. Well, naturally, a few of them have some sort of a double nationality, Like Isaac Bashevish Singer or Joseph Brodsky, but nevertheless: *TEN!!!* Just look it up, and you know the way to the library – some of the books you can surely read electronically on your own computer...and there you go.

Or you could build yourself a boat. In your basement. Perhaps you have noticed my hopelessly intellectual bias: Bit it is really just bogus: I started my working career as a sailor, remember? And I have been occupied in a string of jobs: From a brickwork–plant to a market garden, from a chauffeur with a paper wholesaler–business in my van to a clerk in a bookstore, or working in a car shop, as a bus–driver, truck driver, scrap–dealer, running a hotel ... I very nearly ended up runnning my own kindergarten – instead I wrote this book, like a typical ADD.

The point being that we must not forget the tactical possibilities: There is much relief to be gained from the baking of breads. The knitting of sweaters or painting of walls. Personally, I prefer washing of dishes, ironing my shirts, sewing seams in selected clothing ... NOT. The salvations lies in the acting: "Keeps my mind from wondering," to quote The Beatles. And that is precisely the aim. Or you might study the art of baseball, or macramé, martial arts ... The crucial thing is that all the above mentioned activities lead to a string of other: You have to study history, geography, some philosophy, the art of logistics – or religion for that matter: You will become a self–supporting engine, feeding on your all–engulfing odyssey – to meet with yourself, at last. You suspected as much, didn't you?

The thing is that you will need a couple of activities to keep you busy. Partly in order to prevent your usual state of void–ness to get to you the way it usually does, and partly to keep your body and mind occupied for a while, so in due time you will be able to open up for reflecting upon yourself. That will take some time. But during the first weeks of sobriety, the same old patterns of thoughts will be chasing you: Why do I drink, what am I fleeing from, will they notice that I had a drink yesterday, is there any whiskey left in the jar ... why was I such an ass–hole ...? Better keep your mind from wondering, for some weeks. And equipped with some proper activities, you can keep the bothersome thoughts at arm's length.

In addition to sampling music, practicing my workouts and reading Nobel laureates, I took up skiing. Not as easy in New Mexico or Florida, but water skiing will have the same effect. Conveniently I live just 150 meters from the ski trail, I bought myself some fancy new cross country–skis and the necessary equipment, and every Norwegian know how to ski. We are born with skis on, remember! Which is not the case for most Americans. I know, because I had the hilarious pleasure of teaching how to ski to a fellow pupil in high school, Mike was from San José, California, and was in Norway for one year with an American Field Service scholarship. I taught him how to ski, and simultaneously he learnt how to swear in Norwegian.

But you may remember Bill Koch? Not only did he win the silver medal in thirty–kilometer cross–country skiing in the winter Olympics in Innsbruck in 1976, and the bronze medal in the World Championship in Oslo in 1982, and the World Cup that same year – he also singlehandedly (or rather single footedly) revolutionized cross–country skiing. He invented a new style of skiing, pushing with his poles and advancing by skiing with one of his skis, and floating on the other one. Therefore, he didn't need traditional ski trails, made by trail–preparing snow cats, but rather a well–prepared ground without distinct tracks.

The Scandinavians of course hated his guts and tried to ridicule him and patronized him with talk of the sacred traditions of skiing, the spirit of wooden skis and the lot...but he won! So now we call his style *double–dance* and *skating* and pretend we never heard of Bill Koch or Eric Hayden... but that's another story. I never skated, but now I skied as never before, two rounds before lunch until I fell brutally on the iced surface and broke my collarbone. It was painful, there was some talk about operating on it, but all I got was a sling and strictly impaired mobility for three months. Immobilized in my condition – as a hyperactive teetotalitarian? Very unbearable. Some comfort I gained from the way they characterized my mishap: As a sports–injury.

It outweighed all my inconveniences: *Sports–injury!* I could have kissed that physician. Besides the pure flattering aspects of that expression, it also illuminates some of the comorbid outcomes of the business of keeping yourself busy: Breaches in your deadlock lifestyle inevitably brings about new challenges and experiences, and this new–ness of things is in itself intoxicating. You thought you were a daredevil drinking with your buddies and making a nuisance of yourself – but now: All this entrepreneur business is a sheer thrill in itself. Already you are inside a transition. Your constant feelings of fear and loathing are letting go gradually, eating is fun and you sleep well at night, but still you have this agitation in your belly. But you are hanging in there, I got scheduled exercises for my broken collarbone, and life was interesting. You know; "*With the hip bone connected to the back bone, and the back bone connected to the neck bone, and the neck bone connected to the head bone, Oh mercy how they scare!*"

Not only was I in a situation of transition, but also of recovery. And not only from the accident, but also from my drinking habit. Ironically both situations were self–inflicted, which also illustrates the discharge summary at this phase of my life: I had stumbled and tripped over, and suffered from one short term and one long term situation. I had (a) broken my collarbone while skiing, (b) broken my self–esteem by drinking. None of these situations can be labeled as illness. Both situations are results of your willed actions: You willingly went out skiing and fell brutally – you willingly went out drinking and fell brutally.

So I quit drinking and skiing and went sailing instead. And scuba diving. But that was on the opposite side of the Earth, outside of Queensland, Australia – at the Great Barrier Reef. So hold on tight to the next paragraph!

27

RED SAILS IN THE SUNSET – THE MANUAL AT WORK

How did I end up in Australia? The answer is: Because of my commitment for indigenous cultures. I have already mentioned my assertation on the works of the Sámi author Matti Aikio. Although he did not learn Norwegian until he was grown up, he chose to write in the language of the larger Norwegian society, in times where the unmistakable goal of the Norwegian society was the total assimilation of the Sámi culture – executed from 1890 till 1945. Therefore he was criticized both by his own culture for being a renegade, and from the Norwegian community for not being sufficiently exotic.

And because I'm also a communicating fellow, I have always performed the activity of writing. But in my post–drinking period of hyperactivity, I now decided to raise my efforts: I wrote his biography. One of my prerequisite conditions was that I wrote my master's degree on a couple of his books. I had also lived for a year in the regions he was raised, one of the core areas of the Sámi culture, in the Finnmark region. Plus I had learnt some of their language, history, religion, folklore – the works.

This made me a kind of expert on cultures in transition. Which was the primary focus of the conference "Northern Europe and its Indigenous minority: Pointers for Australia?" Sydney, July 19-22, 2007. The main idea was that the Aborigines, who had been horrendously suppressed by the Australian society, could learn something from the Sámi culture, which is quite a success story, in an indigenous perspective. Present at the conference was for instance the former Chief Justice of the Norwegian Supreme Court and his wife, who at that time was a member of the U.N. Committee on the Rights of the Child. Plus Swedish, Finish, Sámi, and Australian professors and professionals of many flavors. Plus my wife and me. Running with wolves.

I'm trying not to appear bragging, no matter how hard it is. Not to brag. You must allow this one, though: A former drunkard and hopelessly out of work–academic, who had flunked in his first try to land a PhD–degree (have I forgot to tell you? How peculiar): And now – *tataaa!* – I was invited to perform halfway around the globe. I gave a lecture on the works of Aikio, plus I showed a film on the worldwide protests against the damming of Alta, a river that runs all through the Sámi heartland. This film was originally financed and made by the Norwegian Broadcasting, but due to the Norwegian government's and the establishment's persistent will to crush all opposing voices, the film was never shown in Norway. I got hold of it through some obscure channels – it was a huge success. And all the while I was soaking sober!

But there is something seriously important to learn from all this: One will, as teetotalitarian, be able to set a goal that exceeds equilibrium. And for a drinker that is to have a sufficient supply of alcohol at hand at all times. There is no truth that hits harder for an addict than the bottom of a bottle. Only when you are loaded, you'll have thoughts of grandeur and all the pieces of cake you are about to consume in the very near future, it's just a matter of hours, you could make a couple of phone calls right away, mail is for wimps, just need to take out this yawn and then ... you fall asleep. Saved by a kip!

And you wake up in the chair, like so many times – checking status of fluids and time – just in case you need to get hold of some more and where's the nearest off license? Or drugstore? And all your grandiosity down the sink, together with your stale beer... wait a second, that might be the only beer around, have you lost your mind? And in an instance the same old routine clicks back in place, again.

No matter what routines you do have as a habitual abuser of this substance, you know that there are strict limits to what goals you are able to put up for yourself. Mostly, they are about money. Even a modest, but steady intake of alcohol will cost you. And these costs always have top priority. Then comes your reality orientation: You will never embark on a long–term devotion to pursue a goal, unless you can have brakes for drinking. Say, twice a week, and/or each weekend, plus any odd Wednesday ... and there you go. All work and no play make John a naughty boy – and we would not want that.

The truth is, you do not really want to do anything else but drink. Anything else you can accomplish is an extra bonus. All the rest is bogus: Your job, your family, your career, your home ... In your rare moments of reality, you realize that your reality is bogus: Trapped between your awareness about the possibility that you could have done better, and your wish to just keep on floating away in total oblovion forever.

Forever is the key word here. A year of soberness will alter this aspect of a fate fixed forever. The first weeks are crucial. Because it is in these first weeks you actively have to change your fate. As a human being, we are clever in finding the easiest way out when cornered. Therefore we have to simply avoid the usual waterholes, the usual drinking buddies, and situations where drinking is mandatory. Like Friday's wine lottery at work, or coming together at the local with the guys from work after working hours on Fridays, or at the pub after the match, dinner with the in–laws ... Routines fixed forever.

Then there are the talks with your spouse, if you have one. Beware of the bride! I have already warned you: There is almost always a difference between the paroles and the politics. So the urge to get you sober might be laced. Think about it: If your spouse prefers you sober, why hasn't he/she already left you? Or is the person more concerned about the power you unwittingly are bestowing upon them by being mentally incapacitated at times, actually more than half of the time you spend together? This conversation you need to conduct rather quickly, to sort out what your goals are. Hopefully, you really do have mutual goals. But more than likely, you do not.

When all these potential problems around your voluntary abstinence are solved, you will be looking ahead. That's the whole point! If you were not looking for anything, if you are not quivering with unused initiative, with new prospects for your future, with new projects on the stocks, you wouldn't even have bought this book. You have some plans, and now you've got plenty of time at hand. And slowly you realize that now anything might happen! And exactly at this stage of my abstinence, Sydney happened.

But not out of the blue. It is exactly as accidental as how it is with drinking: A crate of beer just happened by. An invitation to a scientific conference on the other side of the planet doesn't just happen upon you. In more sober times you have laid the foundation. Then nothing happened for quite some time; you stopped delivering stuff, you quit showing up in the right places, you went totally off the radar. You were written off. And then you surface, your colleagues remember you, look you up in their archives, and the milieus in which you used to hang out, suddenly are dusting off your ragged reputation – and there you go! Not hard at all. It's like learning how to ski if you are an eighteen–year–old Californian, because it's really like relearning something you already know.

You already know how to walk, you already know how to stand on a surfboard. All you have to do is to combine those activities, you even have a couple of poles to help you catch your balance. And reopening the road to Academia is really like having a refill, only this time it's a refill of knowledge and wisdom. Pardon me – I just couldn't resist that one. And by posing as a ski–instructor I was only returning a favor – my Californian friend Mike had taught me how to play basketball, the American way. We don't do that in Norway — we use a much more timid ball, we have other rules and nothing is similar. In my hometown, we hosted several AFS scholarship–holders, so they were able to form their own basketball team. And I was very proud of being invited as a substitute for their team! I even performed some odd minutes, when they really needed me. But nobody was laughing; neither of Mike, nor of me. As I just asserted: You already know how to walk.

In order to Avoid The Void, you're likely to consolidate your position and standing on your edge of the world. You make yourself available, and make some new contributions. And pretty soon you discover that you are able to offer something others will be asking for. Maybe you just need to change some of the design, or rearrange some of the interior and add some new apps, and in the middle of the night you wake up with this crazy idea... But you have a history of waking up in the middle of the night with this crazy idea, only this time it keeps growing in daylight, and you realize that it is actually doable. Because you do not drown it out with ale. And you let some people know, and suddenly there is an invitation from Sydney in your mail.

My point is that nothing comes by itself. Youve had the capacity and the knowledge, now you also have the necessary stamina. And in addition, you have the joy and playfulness of a person that has been partially unconscious for such a long time, and now you really want to play with the guys, so watch out – here I come! With flying colors!

All the way to Australia, to Sydney, and the Great Barrier Reef, where I took up scuba diving. And the University of New South Wales, where I delivered a couple of performances, as I recollect. By then I had been sober for some months, but without really having planned on staying sober for a year. But now we had to make some mutual decisions, my wife and I. So I told her about my decision: I would stay sober for one entire year. Finally I took them up on their word, this psychologist and that physicist. The last one simply asked me: "Why don't you just quit drinking?" And the first one proclaimed: "Stop drinking for a year, and thence you can drink whatever you like."

I wanted to prove them right. But I didn't want to get my wife's hopes up, without being able to substantiate a promise. So I stopped drinking quite quietly, hoping nobody noticed. And they didn't, but my wife did. Of course. But she didn't want to disturb my intentions, whatever they were. Now when I revealed my decision, she sighed like a small tornado having a puncture in our living room. But she also treated my announcement rather matter–of–factly, and threw in her giving up smoking as a bargain. Which was quite an offer: She smoked at least 30 fags a day. Being a modest smoker myself, with an average of three cigarettes per day, and ten when drinking – and I started at the age of fifteen – I wanted to second that. But then again, this was her challenge.

But to stop smoking before embarking on a journey halfway around the globe, was a smart move. Hours stuck in a plane, other hours stuck in airports, some of them having signs that read "smoking only allowed in designated spaces", as at Heathrow four. And five. Which means exactly nowhere, because they don't *have* any spaces set aside for smoking. I know, because I asked. So in a way it was a relief to get rid of the smoking habit, as my wife did. Only I didn't. Until later on. And experienced that you miss those cigarettes the most when you have them, but are not allowed smoking them. But if it is of any comfort, there is a room for smokers at the airport of Hong Kong.

For me, the timing was perfect for the release of my no drinking scheme: I was on my way to a conference, there would be receptions and dinners and meetings with ambassadors and the whole shebang, it would be an easy solution just to refrain from drinking all together. I decided on blaming it on a health condition – I was past sixty, all sorts of health conditions could be blamed. Everything went smooth as a sponge, only we were never invited when my fellow academics from Norway went pub–crawling. They needed witness–protection...

Clean and sober we arrived in Australia. We visited Uluru, known as Ayers rock. And also her cousin Katja Tura, in the same neighborhood in the desert, not far from Alice Springs. Very majestic, changing colours during the day – but I'm more of a coastal guy, so we headed for the Great Barrier Reef. Here I was tempted with an intensive course in diving, and could I resist the temptation? Not by a long shot. So I went SCUBA–diving, which is an acronym for *s*elf *c*ontained *u*nderwater *b*reathing *a*pparatus. I became a frogman. The first well–known frogmen were the navy diver members of World War II Italian commando frogmen ... and here I go again! But by now you know better – look it up yourself! You could learn a lot both about the history, the apparatus and the gadgets you need, and where to find a firm that actually are dealers of these items, and maybe there are diving classes in the vicinity ...

The point is: I tried it. I prepared for the experience, tried the gear on, crammed the security regulations, learnt how to communicate once submerged, the procedure of emergency calls, how to signal for help, and so forth and so on. And it was fascinating! Creatures of all kinds tapping on my Plexiglas diving mask, steams of colourful fishes in huge crowds, dividing just inches away from the tip of my nose – like standing in front of an advancing flock of reindeers – you know the feeling. And the sensation of the incredible bloom of flowers everywhere and that treasure shining in the distance ... Sorry, I got carried away.

And that I was – I got carried away. And suddenly I had some problems with disposing of my saliva, and the art of breathing in and out in the prescribed way: In short, I was seconds away from panicking. So I signaled to the leader of the pack, we performed a controlled ascent, and I wouldn't miss that experience for my life. But it just wasn't my cup of tea. I usually thrive in tight positions, but this was a bit over the top. Or under the surface... I felt like suffocating. Nevertheless: For a long time I considered taking up scuba diving as a hobby, just to challenge my short–comings, but I declined. Because it was all these other tedious details to take into consideration: Like keeping all that gear in ship shape condition, always knowing the exact and proper pressure of the flasks, the correct mixture of oxygen and whatever is needed – I might be a meticulous man, but this approaches fundamentalism.

So I let go of scuba diving. But at least I tried! Instead we went fishing, visited places of great wonders, the deserts and the jungles, the waterfalls and the wetlands – the whole expedition to Australia was one Magical Mystery Tour. And yes, I almost forgot – we attended the conference of aborigine culture. We heard several lections on multiple topics, and I gave my lecture on the Sámi author Aikio for a limited assembly. But the Norwegian ambassador was present! And then I showed the film for a plenary session. It was met with a huge success – maybe because we had added an animated scene in the final sequence: The dam in the middle of the Sámi region was blown up! Rather warlike – but such a scene was orally suggested in the previous frame by the Norwegian Attorney General in charge at that time, being a passionate salmon fisherman ...

As much as I cherished that reception, the most important incidents took place in the intermissions, as usual. When pausing for a smoke, all the interesting conversations are happening. I met another smoker, a professor from the university of Umea in Sweden. He informed me that it was very possible to get some tutors at his university for writing an assertation for a

PhD ... and would I be accepted? Which I would be, most welcomed, and a fortnight after returning from Sydney (we had a stopover in Hong Kong), I received this phone call from another professor in Umea. A professor in general literature – and the rest is history.

But of course – just not that easy. We returned to Norway, and in solidarity with my wife, I quit smoking as well. Not a great loss for me, but a habit that is harder to get rid off than drinking, believe me! I still fancy a smoke every now and then, but never a drink. I never *want* a drink – I do not long for a beer, or a glass of wine, or a snaps, I simply have lost the passion. I can have a glass or three when it is expected, in social contexts, and therefore I save my drinking for special events, like New Years Eve, or whenever I have to in order not to embarrass others. It's no big deal. One year of teetotalitarian conduct taught me the difference between *to drink* and *getting drunk*.

But my new life wasn't only blueberry pie, of course – it was also a bed of roses. For the time being I am planning to buy myself a small sailboat. I have always wanted one, because I was alone in this boat with my father, and he erected an ore and hoisted a sail – it was a red cloth and not a proper sail, but there we went sailing along, red sails in the sunset ... So a couple of years ago I attended to a sailing course, and now all I needed was a boat of my own, and room for it in a harbor – and then I met with a couple of friends I haven't been in contact with since high school.

But by now I was clean, I invited them to my doctor's dinner and they returned that invitation. On that evening of our gentlemen's supper one of my old friends that dared to restart his friendship with me, also had a place for my ship to be. He lived in our vicinity, close to the fjord of our capital, and you know what? He owned his own wharf. Only he didn't own a boat of his own. If I was interested in using his jetty? I do not even need to include a comment on how opportunities come sailing along, once you are properly equipped. And this is what this book is really about: How to prepare your ship and be properly equipped for the boldest voyage of your life.

I already told you about our travels elsewhere, post–People's Republic of Eastern Germany, when suddenly I felt teletransported to another time and place. That happened to me especially when we, a bit inattentively, visited Rostock, in the middle of former *Deutsche Demokratische Republik*. I had some grave flashbacks, so I had to deal with it: I had to revisit the Soviet Union, and suddenly I was *Back in the USSR*. And as time goes by, in your own pace, the reasons for taking up drinking will dawn upon you, as well. As I told you, I recollected the moment I finally met with my father, in a Soviet criminal asylum... Need I say more? Probably not. In time you will uncover the underlying reasons for your constantly being under the influence, and for this work you might need professional help. I did, but mostly because this ADD–resembling behavior needed to be dealt with. And I never tried any chemical shortcuts, like Ibogaine. There is a bonus chapter at the bottom about chemical treatments. And about why my suggested solution will work:

Why would will work?

But although it took quite some time before I raised my first drink – I had to finish that assertion first – I will withhold that one year of refraining from alcohol will suffice. And it is all a question about Will. Now both my wife and I are enjoying a drink whenever it is fitting and proper.

But we never smoke.

BONUS

28

MEDICAL TREATMENT

I would not recommend that you keep count of the elapsing days, AA–or military service–style: 21 days down, 344 to go, you know the drill. Kind of depresses you, as if there is a prize to be gathered on the day of the first anniversary of your teetotalism. But there isn't. Which could depress you even more. Remember: You are not erecting a totem pole of your newly achieved soberness; you are rather aiming for a position as Queen or King of Cool... And when the storm is finally settling, and you find some adequate techniques to deal with The Void, you will notice this nagging feeling in your guts somewhere. Like a flock of ferrets gnawing away on your endocrine equipment. I've mentioned it before. It's the kind of unbearable tension you felt as a kid when you were visiting a movie theatre for the first time, or a theatre with real people in it, or you are about to enter the merry go round, or you are waiting in vain for The Love of Your Life but you are still Only Sixteen ... and I could go on in infinite: It is that kind of nagging feeling I'm talking about. A bit like when you are sitting in the waiting room at your dentist's ... Only this feeling is with you permanently: You go to bed with it, but it's still there when you wake up. You mistake it for hunger, but after breakfast it's still there, and growing ...!

Those days are gone that you interpret this as Lust for a Drink. It is not hunger, it is not excitement, it is not fear of flying – you can't pinpoint it, only that it is gnawing in your gut and it will not leave. A permanent unease. You are only mildly alarmed, you thought of looking up your physician, maybe you are visiting some medical websites to see if there are remedies you could use to take the tip off this disturbance ... But you decide to dive somewhat deeper into your new line of interest. There was this interesting article in that periodical, or your local music dealer is always full of suggestions, and maybe some extra rounds in my daily exercise will do the trick?

Probably not, but the important thing is not to let this nagging feeling get to you. Because I can reveal: It will pass. And just as un–dramatic as this: Suddenly one day, probably an hour or so after your breakfast, you will realize that it is gone. Or maybe later in the day, you realize that something has happened, but you are unable to nail it; and then, when watching the nine o'clock news on the telly in the evening, suddenly an acknowledgement rises: *The discomfort has left you!* Completely! You try to concentrate, maybe you just forgot how it felt, you try to listen to your stomach, but besides the usual rumbling and sounds of solutions, liquids and fluids floating up and down and hither or thither ... No Nagging. It is silenced, gone, left you completely – and all by yourself you perform a square dance on your parquet. And this I can promise. About halfway through your Year of Voluntarily Soberness the nerve–racking gut–gnawing has left you. For good. Only to visit you when you have escalated to the top of a Merry–go–round. Or the Roller Coaster at Coney Island, which I visited for the first time as a sixteen–year–old sailor...and getting sober is also a matter of conquering your inner sixteen–year–old.

One piece of advice: You are not Only Sixteen any more. But by all means, go drive go–karts for days on end, if that is your choice. As I told you, take up those hobbies that seem the most inviting and agreeable with your life in general – and pursue them. In my experience, they will demand your full attention for a while, and then they just fade away...And you won't miss them. They are only guests very much welcomed, they hang around for a while and help you avoid The Void, and then they are fading into the background, shown a more timid room in your new everyday rattle – or they are simply dismissed.

But in your process of getting sober, one is bound to speculate: Are there probably some medical aids I could use to ease this transition?

And there is. I once happened upon some Valium, but tranquilizers of any kind tend to give such a pleasant intoxication that it actually could develop into a polydrug use. But you could try this "Hangover–blowfish": 1000 mg aspirin, 120 mg caffeine and an acid–neutralizing remedy, approved by America's Food and Drug Administration. Or you could always try Ibogaine.

Ibogaine does reduce alcohol consumption, and the medical authorities have determined that it does so by increasing the level of a brain protein known as glial cell line–derived neurotrophic factor, or GDNF. In a separate study, they demonstrated that GDNF by itself decreases alcohol consumption. (*The Journal of Neuroscience*, NY., Jan. 19, 2005, Vol. 25, No. 3, p. 619). But, as one blogger on the net, who actually was about to take Ibogaine for his third time, publicly confessed: "I actually had serious doubts that Iboga can help me because of the fact that it hadn't prevented the progression of my potential alcoholism in the past. Obviously, this thought became my barrier – so I avoided taking the treatment for the third time for a long period." (Howard Lotsof's *The Ibogaine Dossier*, accessed November 1999, http://www.ibogaine.desk.nl/experience–0302.html).

And that's just the point: Ibogaine eases your abstinence, but it does nothing for your fearful feast of one year's battle with The Void. My position on this topic is quite clear: There are no short cuts to sobriety. Coping with your hangover is always painful. There are several ways to ease those pains, but when those ways appears as short cuts, the really are cul–de–sacs. Or worse: traps of prolonged, and even a diversified or multiplied, abuse. Ibogaine might sober you up rapidly, but you still have some hours of vomiting to live through. And the side effect is what your subconsciousness is whispering: Go on, have some fun ... You can always resort to some more Iboga. This means you have to spend a week in Mexico, or Canada, or some clandestine clinics that all have the same asset in common: They will cost you. Plus you will be able to continue ruining your liver, your kidneys, your family and friends and career and ... What will happen when all your money is spent?

Ibogaine changes nothing, it's just enabling your abuse to continue until your last kidn...money is spent. The medical authorities of the United States, of course, realize this. Therefore they will not welcome this line of treatment: It is more of a detour than a short cut to coping with your drinking problem.

I must admit that I am no fan of chemical treatments at all. And my position is in no way an ideological one. I mean, the Ibogaine remedy is manufactured from natural raw materials: "A naturally occurring psychoactive substance found in a number of plants, principally in a member of the Apocynaceae family known as Iboga (Tabernanthe iboga)." (http://en.wikipedia.org/wiki/Ibogaine). I might add that it is mostly used in treatment of addiction to *opiates*. The reason is that the abstinence here obviously is of a more stern character. But again – Ibogaine would only address the hangover situation. It is of no use when you are ready to face The Void.

One could argue that the reluctance to prescribe sedatives of any kinds, or Ibogaine, is of a semimoralistic shape: You'd better suffer somewhat, in order to realize that your using of certain stimulants really is a *mis*–use, an *ab*use. But the motivation could also be purely physiologic: A prolonged use of any of these harmful substances is exactly that: Harmful to your health. As any physician more than willingly will tell you. There is a better chance you will refrain from further abuse, after a period of suffering. If you simply could take a pill that relieves you from all the pains, you really wouldn't have learnt anything, and you are spoilt meat.

I must add that in the bigger picture I have no objections to any treatments prescribed by physicians. I know that quite a lot are inclined to visit homeopaths, or therapists of a multitude of flavors and choices. And they do get well! While many of us are frowning at these lines of treatment, regarding them as pure quackery. But one should afford to be more generous: You get well from the treatment and those medications you put your trust in. I would never pay a visit to an aroma therapist or a Chinesiologist, but then ... most of our illnesses are partly psychosomatic. So you never know: What kind of therapy would work for me?

However, I will maintain my assumption that there may exist ways of avoiding some of the pains you suffer from sobering up. But there is no easy way to overcome The Void. Although, as I have suggested, there are numerous activities you might choose that would facilitate your rather demanding journey through those muddy waters. But you will prevail, and after one year of chasing or being chased by your foggy or suddenly brilliant memories – you will be rewarded. This I can guarantee. But in different shapes and ways, of course, depending on your individual genesis. In my case, the journey ended in an eternal voyage, as skipper and crew on board my own modest vessel... And this picture could be both symbolic and hard facts, of course. But that does not really matter. And the moment you understand this metaphor, your'e on!

29

WHY *WILL* WOULD WORK

Members of the medical professions will probably disagree with me, when I claim that after one year of total abstinence from alcohol, you can drink whatever you want. I will now argue this position: Why would will work?

The short answer is that you will successfully have transformed your excessive drinking into temperance. But the question is still there: How come? So we have to appear the long & winding answer: Because everything is changed. And here follows a revelation of how this transition is possible, and why it does have these comfortable consequences.

There are complex reasons why physicians probably would oppose to my assertion. They are trained to look for inheritable conditions, and are therefore inclined to regard addiction as such a condition. Psychologists are often of an opposite inclination, by underlining the environmental factors. In the appendix, I will present a list of some literature on these topics. But my main conviction kicks in here: Fighting an addiction with medication, is more or less like David Bowie's singing about "Putting out Fire with Gasoline", in my opinion. I believe in a compound of measures that inevitably will follow a decisive parking of your glasses and bad habits.

First of all: The simple acknowledgment of your abuse will do something to your conscience: Perhaps I really do drink too much? Maybe they are right – my wife, my kids, my colleagues, my friends ... if you still have any of the above mentioned around. And maybe – just maybe: I am wrong. If you DO NOT have any more of the above mentioned around, you are definitely wrong. And as often as not, the affected are more reliable than the abuser. The very minute you really decide to take them up on their pledges, you are way into your transition: It has matured inside your conscience, and now you are, however reluctantly, willing to give your critics some credit, by giving up something of your life style. And what that really means is that you are willing to let go of quite a bite of your narcissism.

Bear in mind that I am neither a physicist or psychologist – but they will both agree with the good doctor (that will be me), that an honest effort to stop drinking is a giant step away from positioning yourself at the very center of life's events: You are allowing second opinions. Only later in the process you'll be able to notice that actions and re–actions regarding your decision, are mutual: You will be treated with respect, hope, curiousness ... But also with spite. Many are they who will be gloating if you fail and fall off the wagon.

If it happens: I have to repeat that if you crack during these twelve months, you have to start all over again. Otherwise, you have just changed your pattern into that of a dipsomaniac's. If you have a ball in a dive after having *passed* that year, it is my experience that it doesn't matter. First, because by then you've lost your stamina: You will fall asleep bottles before you usually do. And when you wake up, there is no way you would want another drink. No way. And I am talking out of experience. And second, you have nowhere to go, your "friends" from back then are long gone – in fact, one of them died last winter ... and there you go. If you REALLY do want to reopen that completed chapter, you do have a real death wish. And then I can't help you.

Because, as I have prophesized: After a year of total abstinence, you can drink whatever you want, without ending up abusing the substance. And here follows some of the arguments backing such a statement:

– For many different reasons, you have dropped hanging with your old drinking buddies. And from the same reasons, you never visit those dives anymore. Maybe you have left the city all together; you really do not wish anyone in your neighborhood the pleasance of gloating if you fall: "What did I say? Just a question of weeks before that miserable piece of ... ". No, you do not want that. But they are all so desperately hoping for you to fail, it's almost uncivilized not to oblige. They all want to kill a mockingbird. So, moving might help. And you are not fleeing, merely adjusting the parameters for your success.

– Follows from the previous point that you are now engaging in new types of conversations with a new type of participants. Not only beer, football and birds and football and birds and ... but all types of topics, with all types of people. Maybe even with your family! If you still do have one. At first, you really do not want to, because you are not really interested – they tend to be talking about anything at all but you! Then maybe you are beginning to get some foul thoughts that maybe you are not the centre of the universe, but then you decide that well, this is interesting anyway! Which is a side effect of that grave decision you have already made, to quit drinking, which actually opens up for the possibility that there are other people around as well. And besides, your buddies were all really also only talking about themselves – you might as well engage in a monologue with a row of roosters.

– And after a while, you are appreciating your talks and conversations and arguments with real people, which means that your narcissism is shrinking into manageable proportions. Which means you are really enjoying other people's company, your work, your family ... LIFE, as many of us know it, with certain spells of happiness every now and then. And the rest of the time you are content. More or less. And that is really the Essence of Life: More or Less.

– Therefore, you have taken up some new activities, some of them rather frantic as a result of the transition you are in the middle of. Most of these activities will not stick, some others will grow, but you are focusing on other enterprises than Booze & Co. In short: You're focusing! And then you notice things, make new decisions about likes and dislikes: You are about to furnish your own version of Reality. And the things you are doing isn't just pastime between work & play, it engages you. One way or the other: It engages you. Which means you are in the middle of a dialectical process of evolution: You are changing your conduct, and so your environments are reacting to your changes and vice versa. And this process is irreversible. If you need proof, just visit your old dungeon, have a soft drink and stay until your old compadres are starting on their third pint for the night. You really ought to, if you can bear staying there that long.

– Of course there are some chemical and physiological processes involved in this transition. But mostly of a friendly kind: Your sleep is improving, as well as your appetite – for the first time in ages you are really enjoying a meal! And when you read, you remember things and you actually do have a recollection of that film you rented last night that you really wanted to watch, but usually you don't remember naught. Still you have some discomforts and malaises that could be easily mended with ... But you so enjoy your new way of living, that you decide to wait it out – maybe there's a drink waiting for you at the other end of this *annuus horribilis*.

But there isn't. That is, there may be a drink for you there, but you simply don't want it. Why? Because no person in his right mind would trade the polyphony of feelings from being alive with a shot of a sleep inducing remedy. Admissions are appropriate: If you still really want to get drunk, you need to see a doctor. He might advice you a long–term therapy with someone you trust. And can afford.

If your health is about average, if you are not bothered with certain physiological problems (like digestive, muscle–related, sleeping problems) that need to be attended to, after a while you will realize that you are actually re–born. A trifle too pompous, perhaps? Nevertheless, it iss a precise description of Life at the moment, according to You. And there is quite an ordinary explanation to this phenomenon, as well: Drinking and thoughts about all aspects regarding the substance and ingestion of said substance including financing of said ingestion is no longer the one and only item on all your schedules ...You read me? Alcohol is no longer on top of every list you used to make:

- Shopping-list: Sufficient
- Timetable: The in-between drinks, when do I have to stop etc.

- Schedule: Remember getting sober to the meeting on Friday!
- Treasure-maps: The brandy is in the saddlebag in the garage this week (better move/empty the one x-tra in the roof drainage – it might rain!)
- Intermissions: Matinee on Thursday!

... And this sad list of lists could be prolonged. But now you will actually be able to indulge in the matinee, you don't have to cancel the meeting on Friday, the roof drainage won't flood and you can afford to surprise your spouse with tickets to a late show one night, well knowing that you won't end up snoring in the chair. At home. When your spouse is trying to locate your last drop of brandy in the saddlebag.

To put it bluntly: When it comes to alcohol, you are rather listless. And the consequence of the emptiness, the void that alcohol is leaving in your existence, is that you have got plenty of time to relish other aspects of the same existence: You are enjoying Life because you are busy doing other things. And thereby I can assert that you are reborn: You are re–instated in the everyday life with all its tedious, challenging, touching, embarrassing, staggering details. And The Void. You are stuck with it for some time, you take up some activities and appear somewhat hyperactive, but at the same time you discover how much you enjoy all those details, all the random conversations and sudden encounters in the metro, at the library, collecting the kids or scolding the manager of the hockey–team ... If only you knew how you miss this!

But The Void is gnawing your guts out, but hang in there! Because after some time, half a year maybe, it simply evaporates. As I already have told you: Suddenly, or rather modestly, it's all gone. And so are most of your so–called comorbide nuisances connected to sleep, digestion and other bodily functions. Every individual must seek relief for their scourges, from the sources they have confidence in. But if there isn't something serious the matter with your health, you will reach the instant where you want to learn more about the underlying reasons for your former abuse.

After I had faced The Void, after the gnawing ferrets in my bowels had left them alone I was ready to turn around and face my stalkers: Whatever dark shadows that were following me day and night, and only kept the distance when I was loaded. And eventually you will find your trigger, even if you may need some help. I found my trigger in the Soviet Union. Voluntarily, I maneuvered myself into splendid isolation, and did what it took to get a conversation with my dad: It was even monitored, translated, and taken down in shorthand!

Somewhat over the top, but I had to resort to drastic means – to blow up the gates of my childhood. In spite of what many from the medical professions are claiming, drinking habits are for the most founded during the four earliest years of an individual's life span. They are often, but not always, living with their models, when it comes to the developing of most of our behavior. Instead of provoking a feud between professionals, they ought to listen to me, a professional drinker: Every abuser do have to confront one's Inner Soviet, and empty all those Gulags inside.

That was what happened with me: Years after the Soviet incident, even after my father's death, I needed to understand the extraordinary drivers of my life. And when my subconsciousness was playing tricks on me, giving me unpleasant flashbacks from suppressed memories when holidaying in former Eastern Germany, I had a breakdown. Rostock gave me the creeps, and Prora smelled like Kuybyshev, the prison in Leningrad for mentally deranged where I spent some time.

Whatever shape or form, you will have an encounter with crucial moments of your life. But that might just be the starting point for your further excavations in your mind and memory. In my case I really was in search of my father, who came, but why did I want to see him, about what? And where was he in my childhood? And my mother? Why was I so heart–wrenchingly abandoned? *A la recherche de temps perdu* – and it might never end. And in this process I ended up in a penitentiary.

With a little help from my friends, and my father, and my defense lawyer, and politicians, and gentlemen of the press – I was released. But it is an interesting piece of fact that quite a large part of drug & alcohol abusers are in and out of jails, correcting camps, institutions of all kinds and flavors – are these people really in need of a home? Or are they unable of living in certain environments? I'm speculating here, but most of the substance abusers are unable to take care of themselves. They lack The Will.

I managed to muster my reservoir of Will. Then I willed myself to keep away from drinking for a year, took up my career and participated on a conference in Sydney, Australia, where we introduced *Pointers for the*

Aborigines. I proved to myself and everybody I knew that even if you cannot change your character, you could alter your conduct. Then I finished my degree as a doctor of philosophy in Sweden, and my conduct might serve as a pointer for every individual who wants to abandon one's bad habits.

30

SUMMARY

Nobody drinks out of lust, or desire. First, drinking alcohol meets certain social expectations. And most of us do not have a problem with that. There are cultures that ban the intake of alcohol, like the members of the Laestadian congregations of the northern regions of Norway, and especially amongst the Sami and the Kvens. But that also happened to my relatives that moved to the States during the depression of the 1920's, and returned as Mormons. They weren't even allowed to enjoy coffee! But as one of my uncles proclaimed, in moments of need: "Please put on the Lutheran kettle!"

Water is drunk out of need. All other beverages are supposed to enrich the tastes and the sensation of drinking. And some of the liquids are intoxicating. And therefore we are enjoying alcohol: Beer because it has a cooling and thirst–quenching effect, wine because it enriches the tastes of food, champagne because of its sparkling behavior, often matching our own sparkling state of mind: New Years Eve, whenever we win Le Mans... But otherwise, coffee or tea, or plain water is usually our preferred beverage. Because alcohol doesn't taste good. If you are thirsty, you'll prefer anything to alcohol. The ones claiming that vintage wine beats everything are vain and pretentious.

Just admit it: You prefer coke to bourbon, coffee over a drink and water over Mosel. And I haven't even mentioned the instrument of bloating present here: Being able to appear as a connoisseur of fine wines, is considered as *très* posh. But none of this is of any importance for those of us that develop a problematic relationship with alcohol. We really don't care, as long as it is alcohol. We try keeping up appearances, but all the while we do not mind of which brand the Brandy is – as long as there is any Brandy at all. We take what it gives. And now it's upon time we demonstrate that we've got what it takes to master alcohol. We are on the road to dethrone Master Alcohol.

Just to sum up this factor: Drinking alcohol is primarily a social act. And it is quite a paradox that the culmination of a social gathering is to induce oneself collectively with a sleeping agent! There are strict rules regulating what you ought to drink where and at what time – and in what circumstances, to what dishes – and last but not least: How *much* you can ingest. The social acceptance for how to appear under the influence is rather restrictive, as is the condemnation of breaking these rules. So most of us are rather careful not to break those rules – we drink what we are served, and are met with some giggles if we get a bit tipsy in public, but you are forgiven. Until the next time, when the giggle is a bit less heartily until you end up with the bottle in a paper bag.

Then there is a good chance you will get a suspicion of developing an addiction. And if so, you're offered the explanation that you are born that way, your addiction is hereditary. But what if there are no abusers among your relatives? In that case, you are born with a *disposition* for addiction, and your only salvation is total abstinence for the rest of your life. I have been challenging this line of explanation. First of all, there are many definitions of the concept of *alcoholism*. The one definition molded in the image of Alcoholic Anonymous is characterized by (a) an acquired increased tissue tolerance to alcohol; (b) adaptive cell metabolism; (c) withdrawal symptoms and craving; and (d) loss of control – a definite progression from psychological to physical dependence, accompanied by behavioral deterioration.

In my opinion, this definition is somewhat deterministic and inaccurate. It does not differentiate the substances, and it does not problematize the concept of *addiction*. In my opinion, one has to differentiate between substances: Tobacco when smoked is addictive, even if it is tough work getting addicted: You start with puking. But when you are properly addicted, that addiction is hard to get rid of. Snuffing and chewing tobacco is also addictive, but easier to quit. Neither cocaine nor marihuana are physically addictive, but the *habit of using* might be. As is the use of all of the other hallucinogens. And the same can probably be said about the industrially produced chemical *speed* substances, like amphetamine – originally an *upper*, but also used in the treatment of ADD–patients. It's a stimulant of the central nervous system, deriving you of sleep and the feeling of hunger, and the use of this substance can really be hard to comprehend. For those individuals suffering from severe impatience, one could resort to the angry cousin methamphetamine, activating the psychological reward system by triggering a cascading release of dopamine in the brain.

Which brings us back to the starting point: Is the addiction of a physical or habitual kind? I mean, the intake of sugar is also activating the dopamine in our brain, ehich makes us feel good – but we have to limit our intake by the use of our will. And how about crack? I'm told that *crack* is creating an almost instantly addiction – a habit that likewise is almost impossible to get rid of. Crack, however, is the basic salt form of cocaine, and therefore a natural substance. But in these discussions, the ecological approach is of no consequence.

Then we have all the other opiates: Heroin, opium, methadone, codeine, vicodin (the favorite of Dr. House) and Sister Morphine. She was a legal substance way into the 1950's, the use and abuse of certain substances are always also a matter of politics and legislation: You can buy and smoke hashish publicly in Amsterdam, whilst pushing the same stuff in Norway can give you a sentence up to fifteen5 years in prison. In California you can buy marihuana for medical use, and in Switzerland even the purchase of heroin is regulated by the state. So there you go.

But is alcohol addictive? Arguments both pros and cons could be heard, but I will maintain that when it comes to alcohol, it is mostly The Void that is addictive – your fear of being stuck with your own hunting thoughts that lead you to excessive drinking in the first place. I will also claim that it is not the crave for more that is leading you on, like with heroin – but rather your daily choice between two evils: Either take the abstinence; with vomiting, sweating, lack of sleep, the works. Or take the relief: Have another drink; with vomiting, sweating, lack of sleep until you faint. If you choose the abstinence, it will take you five days to get "well", clinically. If you choose the relief, you will end up dead in the matter of some time, depending on the rapidness and quantum of the intake – because then you are really *Leaving Las Vegas*. But like the role of actor Nicolas Cage demonstrated in that film: It was hard work and a strong and persistent will that finally brought him where he was really heading.

But, engaging your Will, you will not end up in the morgue as a result of uncontrolled intake of alcohol. There is a serious medical and academic debate going on about how to best control the using of alcohol and thus prevent the occurrence of abuse. The ruling definition is that "alcoholism is a progressive disease that ends in abstinence or death" (Vaillant 1983), while others argue that modest drinking behavior can be developed successfully (Duckert 1993). A list of suggested readings will follow as an appendix. I have my doubts whether training an abuser of alcohol to moderate the intake will be successful – most of the persons at risk already are enjoying a moderate intake, according to themselves. This might apply for abusers admitted to a clinic – but then they have already entered some detox–program. And besides, clinical surroundings will most efficiently overrule the administration of one's free will.

I believe that avenues that are more drastic are more promising, in a longer perspective: To initiate an act of will, which includes planning and reorientation – and offers the satisfaction of administering your own renovation of your Life & Reality in your own right. By meager means, with persistence, shedding a lot of sweat, trying, brooding, contemplating on what actions you would like to plunge into – and suddenly the revelation when The Grudge has left your belly. And then, for the first time, you start to believe that this is doable.

But how did you get there? Or for you fresh readers: How do you get there? Let me take you back in my tracks: How I left my last drink in my regular dive and plunged into one year of teetotaler conduct that developed into temperance. To obtain this, I give you a schedule for coming to pragmatic terms with your drinking.

First – You need to wake up: You need to acknowledge that you are drinking too much. There is a scale for your deterioration from a social position and into the gutter. You have to admit that you are on a slippery slope. Just look into the mirror! Need I say more? No, because the abuser knows, it's just so hard to admit. But once you have confessed, there is hope! And don't listen to this once a drunkard, always a drunkard–refrain.

Second – Get sober. This will take you five days, just enough time to read this book. And then: Read it once more. Now you are ready!

Third – Think it through once again. Then make a decision: Yes, I can! For one year, I will not touch a drop of alcohol. I will not falter. If I fall off the wagon, I do have to start all over again. You have to consider if you have anyone you can confide in – other than the one you might be living together with – a friend, a colleague, the vicar? It might be too early to inform, and thereby stress, the relationship with a spouse. But you need someone to talk to.

Fourth – The Void is testing you. After some weeks you will notice the eternity of free time at your hands, your legs are taking you on endless hours of walking, but your head doesn't know where you are heading. You are running away from something. You need to slow down, turn around and face the follower. But there's no one behind you, so you have to face The Void. You are now nearing the center of your transition, and at this point I found myself in a cell in the Soviet Union. You are about to reveal the reasons for your running away from yourself and your life. You are entering the dimension that is the

Fifth – Testing The Void. Although, or rather because, you have got a lot on your mind, you need to take up some activities in order not to be pondering too much over your sad life & tragic fate. You are getting slightly hyperactive, and I suggest that you follow those intentions that first comes to your mind: Engage in practical hobbies and pastime, you may take up a lot and abandon most of them after a while, but some of them will stick around for quite some time.

Sixth – Now is the time of informing your family, your spouse, friends, working colleagues – anyone you think should know about this self–inflicted intervention in your life. You have to be careful with your spouse: Do they really want you to quit drinking? This question is also one of power, or rather the balance of power: Abusing alcohol may be harmful to your relationship – but also stopping the abuse might become harmful to your relationship. Someone's gotta give. Great delicacy is requested in your handling of this situation. Is your spouse a helper – or an antagonist?

Seventh – Craving and loss of control: You have to get rid of your buddies. By *buddies* I mean those guys you only share one activity with – *specifically*, – drinking. You will experience that this is most likely the case, and then it is good riddance! I can guarantee that you won't be missed, and if you show up at your local, ordering a non–alcohol beer, they all wish you dead. At least somewhere else. Or they want to test you, so they can gloat when you fall – and they will wait for that fall for the rest of your life. Don't visit that well.

Eight – You might have to change the Well. By that I mean that things would probably go smoother if you moved out of town. A lot of different factors will be at play here – so you have to take all the upsides and downsides in consideration. Good luck! It could be easy, but also extremely difficult.

Ninth – Finally you are starting to harvest some benefits from your hazardous adventure: You are really enjoying your re–awakened and re–started faculties: You are noticing your environments, not just your liquid situation. On this stadium of your transition you are developing from a solitaire to a mutual conduct of your everyday life – you are ditching your inner Narcissus by pounds each day. You are transforming into a more interactive person: "No Man is an Island." (John Donne, *Meditation XVII*, 1624). The Void is letting go – sleep has found you! And all this thrilling food! And suddenly: The Gnawing Ferrets are gone!

Tenth – In the same Meditation, that same ancient Englishman also stated that because he was involved in humankind, you should "never send to know for whom the bell tolls; it tolls for thee." And the bell tolls for you – now you can just linger in all your new achievements as time goes by; and before you know it, a whole year has elapsed. And do you really want a drink? My personal experience is that alcohol has lost all of its attributed features: You are left with the social significance of the substance. And life is full of social situations demanding a drink: Fridays' wine lotteries, diners, supper with your subordinates or seniors, boat owners can tell you about the anchor drams – my father even saluted us with a bedside snaps, first thing in the morning on Christmas Day and Man – I need a drink! Did I stand a chance?

You do not want to spoil the party by not drinking in public. You take part in the suggested toasts, raising the correct glass at the proper times, while you cherish the gentle feeling of relax that say, four glasses of wine and one cognac might provide during one long evening. Every once in a while. It works for me! Because the overall aim is to reserve a modest and balanced position for the pleasure of enjoying a drop of alcohol every now and then. And at the same time prevent you from compensating drinking with other activities such as gambling, excessive sporting, embracing religions or other lifestyle organizations – instead of enjoying the will to choose among the fabulous diversity of Life outside of your bottle.

My critics will claim that a drink is the first thing you crave after one year of abstinence. And you might. But my guess is that you won't. And why not? Here's my experience: You do not want to have a drink. Because this year of totalism does not feel like a prison: It isn't like you are having a countdown for the hours to go before your release. To be frank: You haven't planned for this, there is no welcome home party, no take care of yourself–ceremony – it's just another usual day. My guess is that you haven't even marked a date in your pocket planner, or iPhone or anything at all – because you already have outgrown it.

Of course I could be wrong, because empirical data backing my allegation is hard to come by: It's almost impossible to have such a project endorsed, or significant funds raised for research on peoples intake of alcohol in their spare time. Therefore, I might be wrong. But you are by now a changed person. Not in the sense that your character is fundamentally changed, that can hardly be achieved even in a long term therapy – but you have changed your *conduct*. You have dismissed some of your buddies, your favorite waterholes, maybe changed job or even moved – and how about your spouse?

The bottom line is that you have changed a whole range of habits. And in that process you have been focusing above the brim of the glass – and quite clearly you can see, and hear, and even smell! not to mention taste the incredible range of all items large and small that creates your world, and Consider the lilies, how they grow: Suddenly you are satisfied with growing into the new world of yours.

Of course you might have problems of physical or psychological nature, which need to be attended to. No wonder, you have also been abusing both Psyche and Soma for quite some time. But since alcohol no longer is at the center for all your attention, you are able to notice that help is to be found all around you: Your inner Narcissus is no longer blocking your view. And that's why you won't run for the nearest drugstore to purchase some liqueur. But in due time, there you are with a drink. It took me quite some time before I reached to my first drink, we actually went to a training camp in Spain my wife and I (yes, she's still there!) My doctoral supper was approaching, and I didn't want to make a fool of neither my professorial company, nor of myself. So we dined my wife and I, we went through the whole ritual: A sherry for starters, white wine with the fish, a glass of claret with the beef and then port with the cheese. Then a *Gran Duke d'Alba* with the coffee. And then: Strolling home through the warm Mediterranean night, sleeping like a million dukes...

And never felt better the day after. Only a bit puzzled: This is really how I have always wanted it: Having a couple of beers with the buddies after work once or twice a week, a glass or three in social settings without making a nuisance of myself and regretting ever after. And another thing that puzzled me: The taste. I mean – alcohol tastes like crap. You only drink it because you have to, it is expected, there's a set of social rules and you do want to fit in. You may disagree, but that's not the point: Alcohol is no big deal! And you can handle it. That's the big deal.

I would like to conclude with my theory: During this year of abstinence, you have mustered a will you were not aware of having at your command. You have rediscovered your former interests and ditched a few, but added others. And after having conquered The Void, you have plenty of time to cherish the simple pleasures of life and really cherish them – how about all the time you can spend alone with your grandchildren? Whom you might not even be allowed to see, or left alone with – you might not even be around yourself!

And since Narcissus has been forced into the basement, you have discovered the company that humility is offering: Gives you a reassuring sense of the proportions of reality. Which provides your everyday life with a certain balance and equilibrium, plus you are eating & sleeping well and regularly. And having fun forever and a day – you are reading books, writing whatever is needed and watching films and plays and remembering everything afterwards and Life is a miracle! And this miracle is a more regular lifestyle with dining and whining as scheduled, work & pleasure in reasonable proportions, more tranquility and less drama: You are growing into a holistic entity, you are enjoying your own free will – you are no longer under the influence.

APPENDIX – LITERATURE

Abrams, D.B. & Niaura, R. (1987). "Social learning theory of alcohol abuse" in Blane, H.T. & Leonard, K.E. (eds.): *Psychological Theories of Drinking and Alcoholism*, New York: Guilford Press.

Adams, D. (1979). *The Hitchhiker's Guide to the Galaxy*, London: Pan Books).

American Psychiatric Association. (2000). DSM–IV: *Diagnostic and Statistical Manual of Mental Disorders – TR version*.

Beck, A.T., Wright, F.D., Newman, C.F. & Liese, P. (1993). *Cognitive Therapy of Substance Abuse*. New York: Guilford Press.

Berg, I.K. & Miller, S.D. (1992). *Working with the Problemdrinker. A Solution–Focused Approach*. New York: W.W. Norton & Company, Inc.

Castaneda, C. (1968). *The Teachings of Don Juan: A Yaqui Way of Knowledge*. Los Angeles: Simon & Shuster.

Chick, J. (1985). "Some rquirements of an alcoholic dependence syndrome". In Heather, N., Roertson, I. & Davies, P. (eds.): *The Misuse of Alcohol; crucial Issues in Dependence, Treatment and Prevention*. London: Croom Helm.

Davies, R. (2004). *Christian Slaves, Muslim Masters: White Slavery in the Mediterranean, the Barbary Coast and Italy, 1500–1800*. Ohio State University: Palgrave Macmillan, Colombus.

Davis, W. (1985). *The Serpent and the Rainbow.* New York: Simon & Schuster.

Duckert, F., Koski–Jännes, A. & Rønnberg, S. (ed.). (1989). *Perspectives on Controlled Drinking.* Helsinki: NAD–publication No. 17.

Edwards, G. & Gross, M.M. (1977). *Alcohol Related Disabilities.* Geneva: World Health Organization.

Fingarette, H. (1989). *Controlled Drinking. The Muth of Alcoholism as a Disease.* Berkeley: University of California Press.

Heather, N. & Robertson, I. (1981). *Controlled Drinking.* London: Methuen.

Heather, N. (1989). "Controlled drinking treatment: Where do we stand to–day?" in Løberg, T., Nathan, P.E. & Marlatt, G.A. (eds.). *Addictive Behaviors: Prevention and Early Intervention.* Amsterdam: Swets & Zeitlinger.

Hodgson, R.J. & Rankin, H.J. (1982). "Cue exposure and relapse prevention" in Hay, W.M. & Nathan, P.E. (eds.). *Clinical Case Studies in the Behavioral Treatment of Alcoholism.* New York: Plenum Press.

Institute of Medicine (1990). *Broadening the Base of Treatment for Alcohol Problems.* Washington, D.C.:National Academy Press.

Jung, J. (2001). *Psychology of Alcohol and Other Drugs. A Research Perspective.* Thousand Oaks: Sage Publications Inc.

Kennedy, W P. (September 1961). "The Nocebo Reaction", *Medical World*, Vol.95, pp.203-205.

Marlatt, G.A. & Gordon, J.R. (1985). *Relapse Prevention: Maintenance Strategies in the Treatment of Addictive Behaviors.* New York: Guilford Press.

Milton, G.W. (23 June, 1973). "Self-Willed Death or the Bone-Pointing Syndrome", *The Lancet,* pp.1435–1436.

Purdue, L. (1992). *The French Paradox and Beyond: Live Longer with Wine & the Mediterranean Lifestyle.* London: Renaissance Press.

Roizen, R. (1987). "The great controlled–drinking controversy" in Galanter, M. (ed.). *Recent Developments in Alcoholism vol. 5.* New York: Plenum Press.

Royal College of Psychiatrists. (1986). *Alcohol – Our Favourite Drug.* London: Tavistock Publications.

Rubel, A.J. (July 1964). "The Epidemiology of a Folk Illness: Susto in Hispanic America", *Ethnology,* Vol.3, No.3, pp.268-283.

Vaillant, G.E. (1983). *The Natural History of Alcoholism: Causes, Patterns and Paths to Recovery.* Cambridge: Harvard University Press.

Ystrom, E., Reichborn–Kjennerud, T., Aggen, S.H. & Kendler, K.S. (2011). "Alcohol Dependence in Men: Reliability and Heritability" in *Alcoholism: Clinical and Experimental Research,* Vol. 35, No. 9, Oslo: National Institute of Health, September 2011.

www.ingramcontent.com/pod-product-compliance
Lightning Source LLC
Chambersburg PA
CBHW050440290526
45786CB00006B/2094